SCHOLASTIC

Now I Know My ALPHABET Learning Mats

50+ Double-Sided Activity Sheets That Help Children Learn the Letters and Sounds of the Alphabet

Lucia Kemp Henry

New York • Toronto • London • Auckland • Sydney
Mexico City • New Delhi • Hong Kong • Buenos Aires

Teaching Resources

Edited by Immacula A. Rhodes
Cover design by Scott Davis
Interior illustrations by Lucia Kemp Henry
Interior design by Holly Grundon

ISBN: 978-0-545-32061-0

Published by Scholastic Inc.
Printed in the U.S.A.

6 7 8 9 10 40 19 18

Contents

Learning Mats

Learning Mats (continued)

Mat	Skill
53–54	Uppercase N
55–56	Lowercase n
57–58	Uppercase O
59–60	Lowercase o
61–62	Uppercase P
63–64	Lowercase p
65–66	Uppercase Q
67–68	Lowercase q
69–70	Uppercase R
71–72	Lowercase r
73–74	Uppercase S
75–76	Lowercase s
77–78	Uppercase T
79–80	Lowercase t
81–82	Uppercase U
83–84	Lowercase u
85–86	Uppercase V
87–88	Lowercase v
89–90	Uppercase W
91–92	Lowercase w
93–94	Uppercase X
95–96	Lowercase x
97–98	Uppercase Y
99–100	Lowercase y
101–102	Uppercase Z
103–104	Lowercase z

About This Book

Welcome to *Now I Know My Alphabet Learning Mats*! The 104 double-sided mats in this book provide engaging activities designed to help children master alphabet recognition and letter-sound associations. In addition, the systematic format reinforces emerging reading and fine-motor skills while enabling children to work independently.

The interactive, reproducible mats feature appealing art and simple, predictable text to target each uppercase and lowercase letter of the alphabet. Activities include identifying, writing, and matching letters; phonemic awareness, making distinctions between letters with similar sounds or formations; and recognizing letter sounds. The tracing and writing exercises help develop and strengthen fine-motor skills as well as reinforce the shape and formation of each letter. And, as children read and follow directions to complete each mat, they build important word recognition and comprehension skills. To help meet the learning needs of your students, refer to page 8 to see how activities in this book connect to the Common Core State Standards for Reading (Foundational Skills) and Language, as well as the language arts standards recommended by Mid-continent Research for Education and Learning.

Preparing and using the learning mats is quick and easy! Simply make double-sided copies to use for instruction with the whole class, small groups, student pairs, or individuals. The mats are also ideal for independent work, centers, and homework. You'll find that daily practice with these activities builds alphabet recognition and other early literacy skills. Best of all, children will experience the joy of learning as they develop skills that help them grow into more confident, fluent readers.

What's Inside

Each ready-to-go learning mat in this resource targets a specific uppercase or lowercase letter. To use, simply decide on the letter you want to teach, locate the corresponding mats in the book, and make a double-sided copy of the selected mats. The only materials kids need for the activities are crayons or colored pencils. To use, children read and follow the directions to perform each activity. You'll find several activity formats throughout the book, as described below:

Uppercase Letters

- **Trace and Write:** Children trace the uppercase letter and then write the letter on their own without guides.
- **Color-Coded Picture:** Children color each space that contains the target letter as directed and then color the rest of the picture as desired.
- **Identify the Letter:** Children use visual discrimination skills to distinguish the target letter from other similarly shaped letters.
- **Complete the Word:** This fill-in-the letter activity gives additional reinforcement in writing the target letter. Children can read the word to name the picture and practice pairing the letter sound to its printed form.
- **Identify Beginning Sounds:** This activity lets children identify and color items that begin with the sound of the target letter.

Lowercase Letters

- **Trace and Write:** In this activity, children trace the lowercase letter and then write the letter on their own.
- **Identify the Letter:** Visual discrimination skills are reinforced as children distinguish the target letter from other similarly shaped letters.
- **Hidden Picture:** Children identify the target letter and color that space as directed to reveal a hidden picture.
- **Write the Letter:** This activity offers children additional opportunities to write the target letter on their own. Most of the mats also include a picture-tracing component to give children practice in fine-motor skills.
- **Trace and Read:** Children trace a word that begins with the target letter, then read the word and circle other words that contain that letter, building word recognition and comprehension skills.

Helpful Tips

The following suggestions will help you and your students get the most out of the learning mats:

- Complete each mat in advance to become familiar with the directions, art, and response for each activity. If desired, laminate your completed copy to use as an answer key. (Or slip the mat into a clear, plastic page protector.) You might bind all of your answer keys into a notebook to keep on hand for children to check their work.
- Use the mats to introduce new concepts, track children's progress in mastering essential skills, and review concepts already covered.
- Prepare the mats for repeated use in learning centers. Simply laminate the double-sided mats and put them in a center along with wipe-off color crayons and paper towels (to use as erasers).
- Compile sets of the learning mats into booklets for children to complete in class or at home. For example, you might staple copies of mats 1–12 between two sheets of construction paper and title the booklet, "My Book of Letters: A, B, and C."
- The mats are also perfect for instant homework assignments. Send the pages home with children to complete. This is an easy way to reinforce skills covered in class as well as to help keep families informed about what their children are learning, what they've mastered, and where they might need some extra guidance.

Alphabet Learning Mats Reference List

Use this handy list as a reference for identifying pictures that begin with the target letter on the even-numbered uppercase letter mats (the target letter is printed in bold) and checking children's hidden picture activity on the odd-numbered lowercase letter mats.

Mat 2 (A): **a**nt, **a**pple, **a**x, eggs, pan
Mat 3 (a): hidden picture: apple

Mat 6 (B): **b**all, **b**alloon, **b**ear, dog, pig
Mat 7 (b): hidden picture: balloon

Mat 10 (C): apple, **c**andle, **c**at, **c**upcake, pig
Mat 11 (c): hidden picture: cupcake

Mat 14 (D): bear, **d**og, **d**oor, **d**uck, tent
Mat 15 (d): hidden picture: duck

Mat 18 (E): ax, **e**gg, **e**lephant, **e**nvelope, igloo
Mat 19 (e): hidden picture: egg

Mat 22 (F): **f**eather, **f**ish, **f**ox, pig, vest
Mat 23 (f): hidden picture: feather

Mat 26 (G): cupcake, duck, **g**ate, **g**oat, **g**opher
Mat 27 (g): hidden picture: gate

Mat 30 (H): apple, duck, **h**amster, **h**at, **h**ouse
Mat 31 (h): hidden picture: hat

Mat 34 (I): ax, egg, **i**gloo, **i**guana, **i**nstruments
Mat 35 (i): hidden picture: iguana

Mat 38 (J): duck, **j**ar, **j**eep, **j**ellyfish, tent
Mat 39 (j): hidden picture: jacket

Mat 42 (K): dog, gate, **k**angaroo, **k**ey, **k**ite
Mat 43 (k): hidden picture: kite

Mat 46 (L): **l**adder, **l**ion, **l**ollipop, web, yarn
Mat 47 (l): hidden picture: lollipop

Mat 50 (M): bear, **m**itten, **m**ouse, **m**ushroom, net
Mat 51 (m): hidden picture: mitten

Mat 54 (N): mushroom, **n**et, **n**ewspaper, **n**ewt, table
Mat 55 (n): hidden picture: net

Mat 58 (O): ax, **o**live, **o**strich, **o**tter, umbrella
Mat 59 (o): hidden picture: olive

Mat 62 (P): ball, mushroom, **p**an, **p**ig, **p**oodle
Mat 63 (p): hidden picture: purse

Mat 66 (Q): fish, goat, **q**uail, **q**uestion mark, **q**uilt
Mat 67 (q): hidden picture: quilt

Mat 70 (R): **r**accoon, **r**adish, **r**ing, vase, web
Mat 71 (r): hidden picture: radish

Mat 74 (S): cat, **s**eagull, **s**ock, **s**oup, zipper
Mat 75 (s): hidden picture: soup

Mat 78 (T): fish, jeep, **t**able, **t**ent, **t**urtle
Mat 79 (t): hidden picture: turtle

Mat 82 (U): igloo, olive, **u**mbrella, **u**nderwear, **u**nicorn
Mat 83 (u): hidden picture: umbrella

Mat 86 (V): bear, duck, **v**an, **v**est, **v**ulture
Mat 87 (v): hidden picture: V

Mat 90 (W): house, ring, **w**agon, **w**alrus, **w**eb
Mat 91 (w): hidden picture: window

Mat 94 (X): cat, sock, e**x**it, **x**-ray, **x**-ray fish
Mat 95 (x): hidden picture: X

Mat 98 (Y): igloo, wagon, **y**ak, **y**arn, **y**o-yo
Mat 99 (y): hidden picture: yo-yo

Mat 102 (Z): dog, sock, **z**ebra, **z**ipper, **z**ucchini
Mat 103 (z): hidden picture: zebra stripes

Meeting the Standards

Connections to the Common Core State Standards

The Common Core State Standards Initiative (CCSSI) has outlined learning expectations in English/Language Arts for students at different grade levels. The activities in this book align with the following standards for students in grades K–1. For more information, visit the CCSSI Web site at www.corestandards.org.

Reading Standards: Foundational Skills

Print Concepts

- RF.K.1, RF.1.1. Demonstrate understanding of the organization and basic features of print.
- RF.K.1a. Recognize and name all upper- and lowercase letters of the alphabet.

Phonological Awareness

- RF.K.2, RF.1.2. Demonstrate understanding of spoken words, syllables, and sounds (phonemes).

Phonics and Word Recognition

- RF.K.3, RF.1.3. Know and apply grade-level phonics and word analysis skills in decoding words.

Fluency

- RF.K.4, RF.1.4. Read with sufficient accuracy and fluency to support comprehension.
- RF.1.4a. Read grade-level text with purpose and understanding.
- RF.1.4b. Read grade-level text orally with accuracy, appropriate rate, and expression.
- RF.1.4c. Use context to confirm or self-correct word recognition and understanding, rereading as necessary.

Language

Conventions of Standard English

- L.K.1, L.1.1. Demonstrate command of the conventions of standard English grammar and usage when writing or speaking.
- L.K.1a, L.1.1a. Print upper- and lowercase letters.
- L.K.2, L.1.2. Demonstrate command of the conventions of standard English capitalization, punctuation, and spelling when writing.

Connections to the McREL Language Arts Standards

Mid-continent Research for Education and Learning (McREL), a nationally recognized nonprofit organization, has compiled and evaluated national and state standards—and proposed what teachers should provide for their PreK–1 students to grow proficient in language arts. This book's activities support the following standards:

Uses general skills and strategies of the reading process including:

- Knows uppercase and lowercase letters of the alphabet
- Uses basic elements of phonetic analysis (e.g., understands sound-symbol relationships; beginning and ending consonants, vowel sounds) to decode unknown words

Uses grammatical and mechanical convention in written compositions including:

- Uses conventions of print in writing (e.g., forms letters in print, uses uppercase and lowercase letters of the alphabet)

Source: Kendall, J. S. & Marzano, R. J. (2004). *Content knowledge: A compendium of standards and benchmarks for K–12 education.* Aurora, CO: Mid-continent Research for Education and Learning. Online database: http://www.mcrel.org/standards-benchmarks/

Name: ______________________________

Trace. Write.

A A A

Find each **A**. Color that shape brown. Then color the rest of the picture.

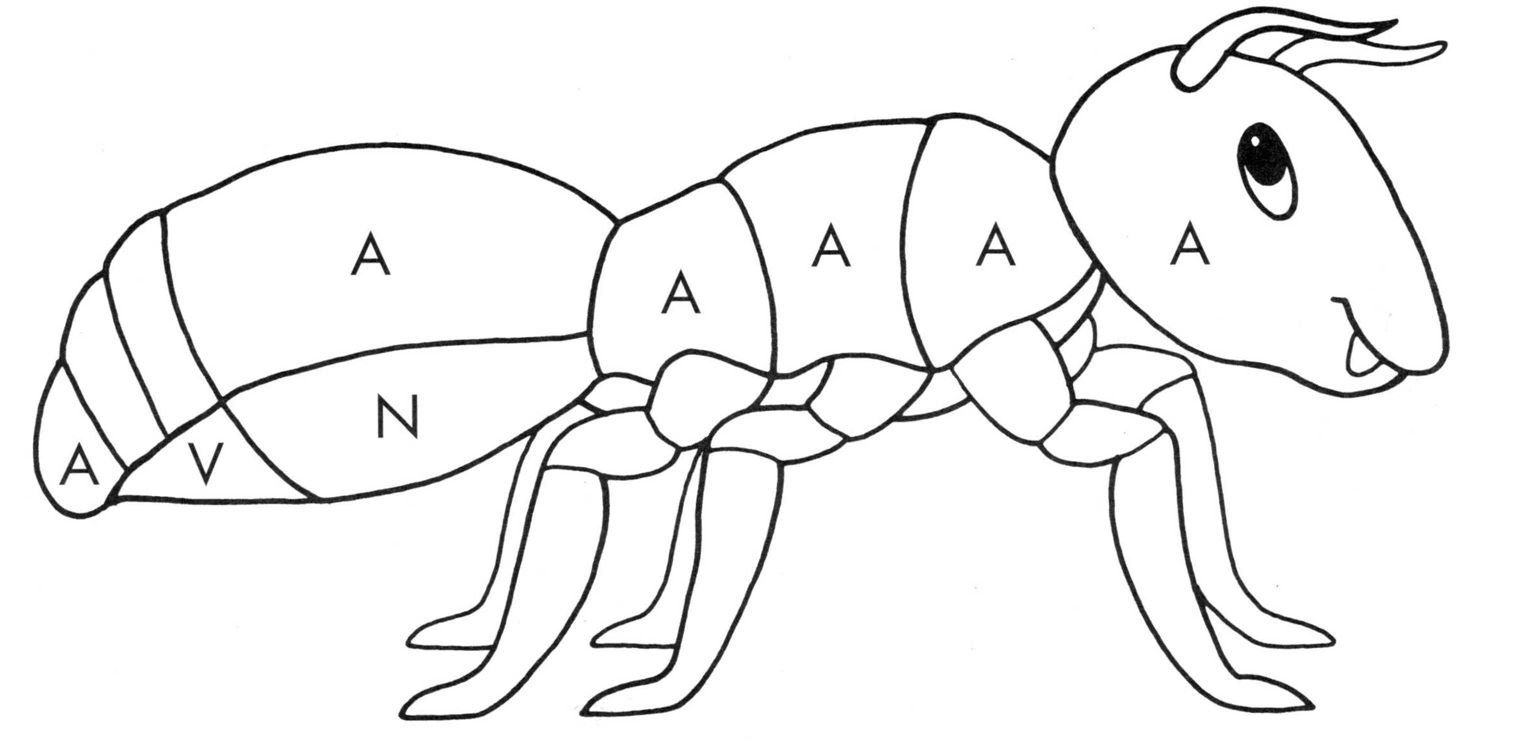

2 Name: ____________________

Uppercase A

Circle each **A**.

A V A X

W A N A

Write **A** to complete the word.

_pple

Color each item that begins with **A**.

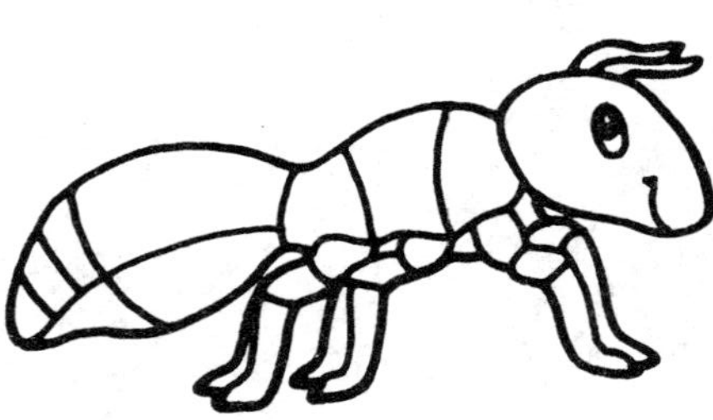

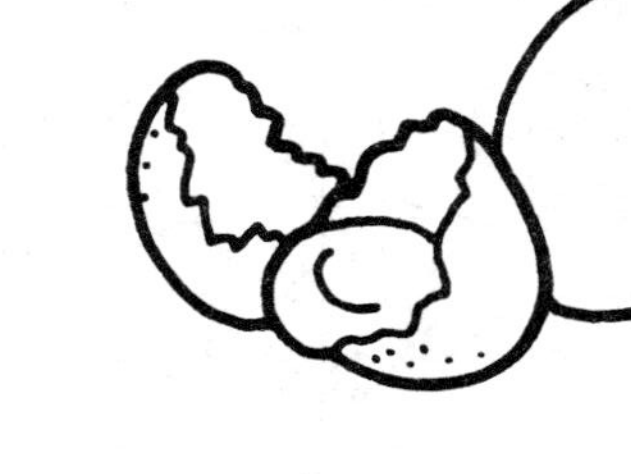

3 Name: ____________________

Trace.

Write.

Circle each **a**.

c a n
d a

Find each **a**. Color that shape red.
Then color the rest of the picture.

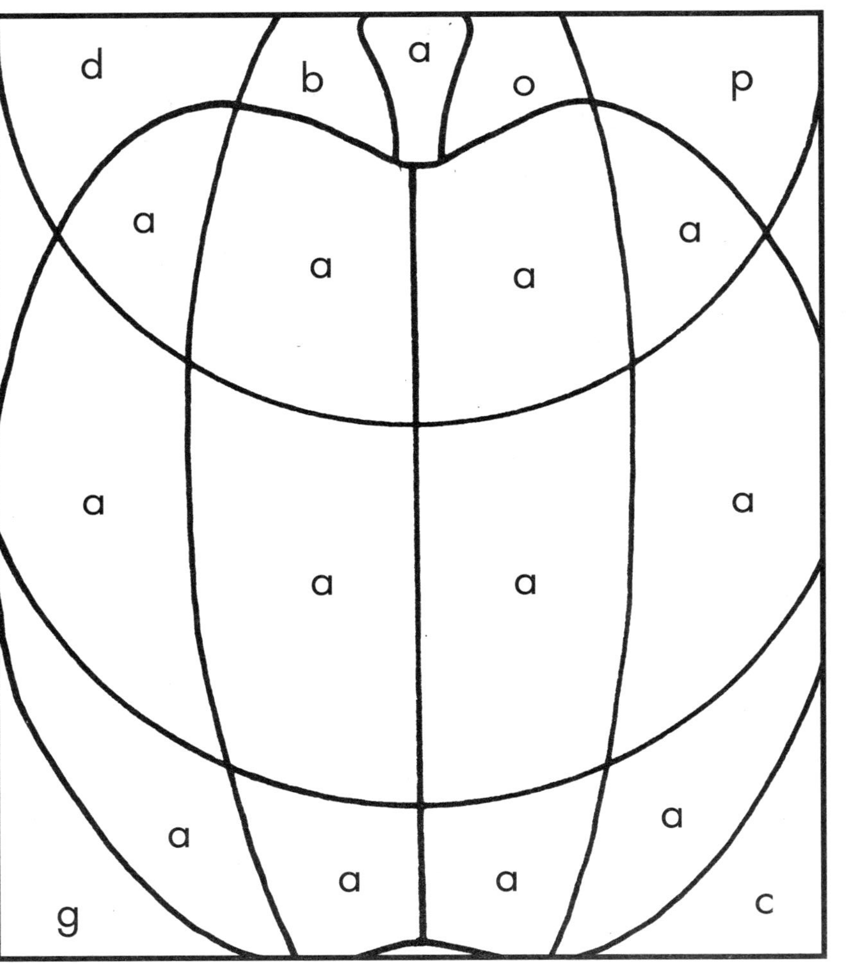

4 Name: ____________________

Lowercase a

Trace each apple. Write **a** on each one.

Trace the word below.
Read the words on the anthill.
Circle each word with an **a**.

ant

an
ant
one
and

7

Name: ______________________

Trace.

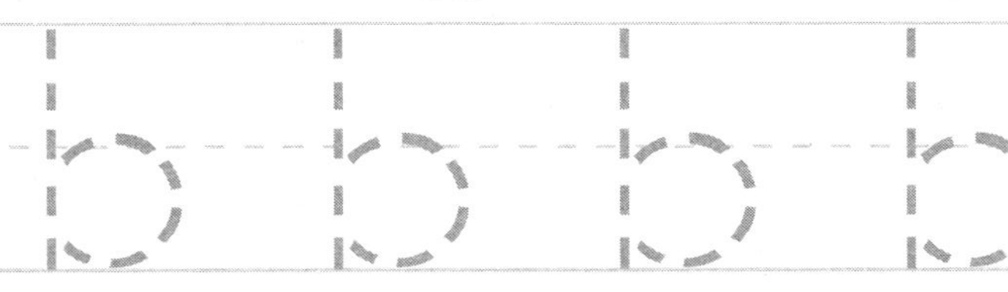

Write.

Circle each **b**.

b d b
b p

Find each **b**. Color that shape blue.
Then color the rest of the picture.

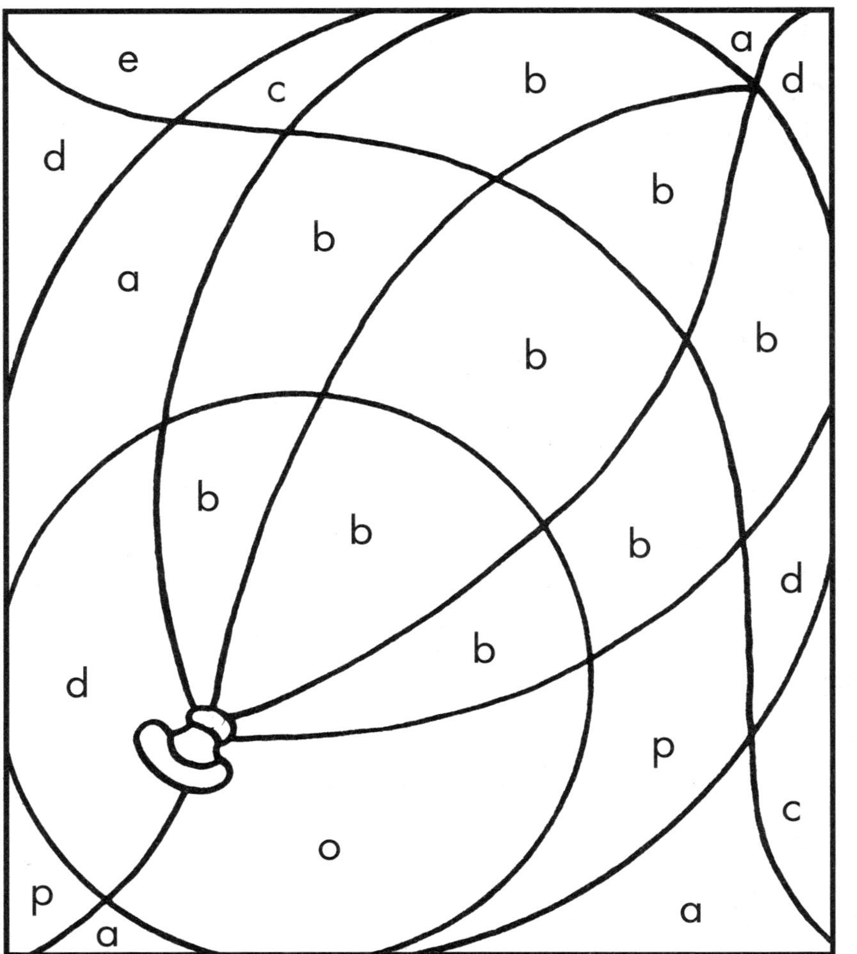

Name: ______________________

Trace each balloon. Write **b** on each one.

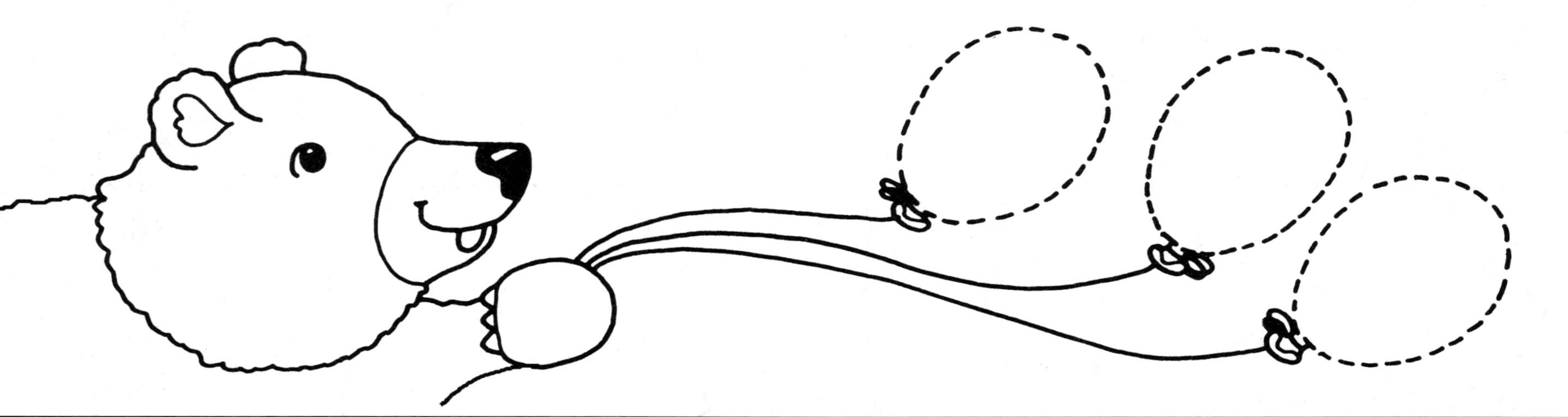

Trace the word below.
Read the words on the balloon.
Circle each word with a **b**.

balloon

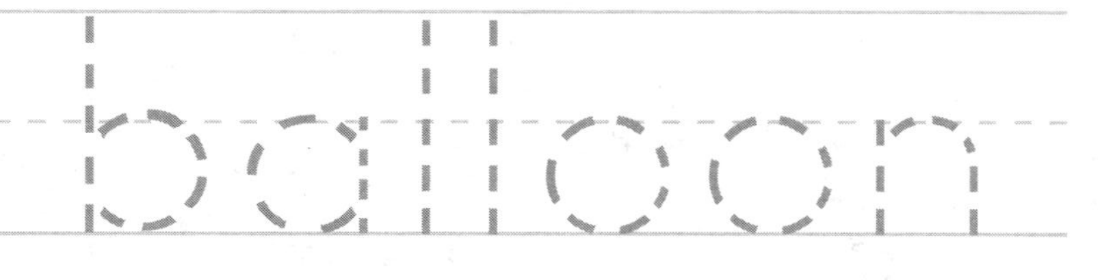

11 Name: ____________________

Trace.

Write.

Circle each **c**.

Find each **c**. Color that shape pink.
Then color the rest of the picture.

5 Name: ____

 Name: ____________________

Trace each cupcake. Write **c** on each one.

Trace the word below.
Read the words on the cupcake.
Circle each word with a **c**.

cupcake

13 Name: ____________________ Uppercase D

Trace. Write.

D D D

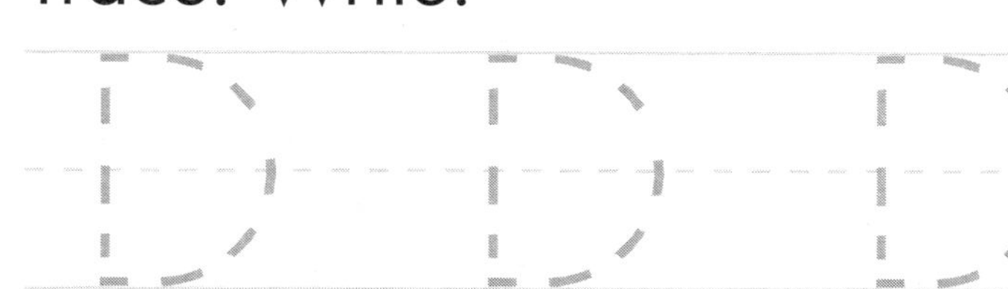

Find each **D**. Color that shape black. Then color the rest of the picture.

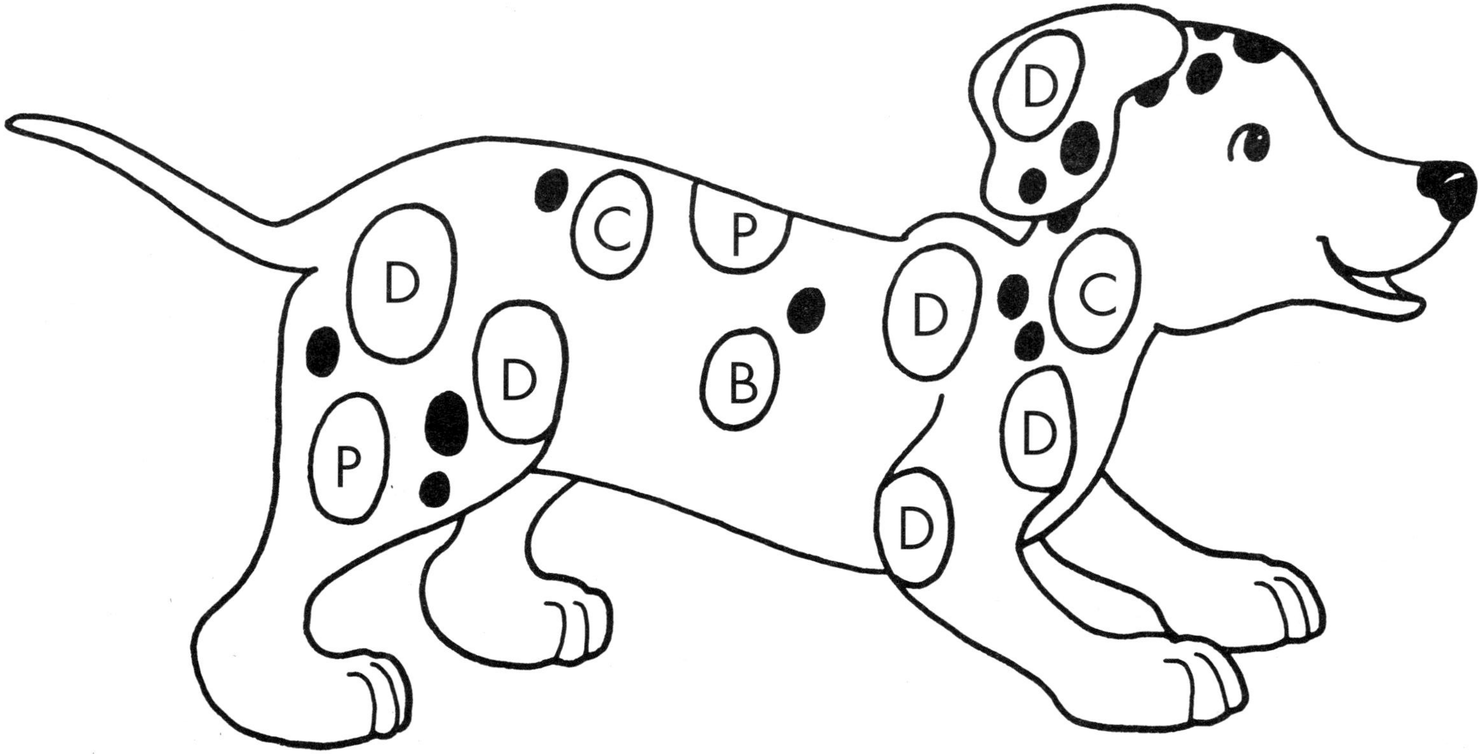

14 Name: ______________________________ Uppercase D

Circle each **D**.

D P D G

C D B D

Write **D** to complete the word.

_og

Color each item that begins with **D**.

Name: ____________________

Trace.

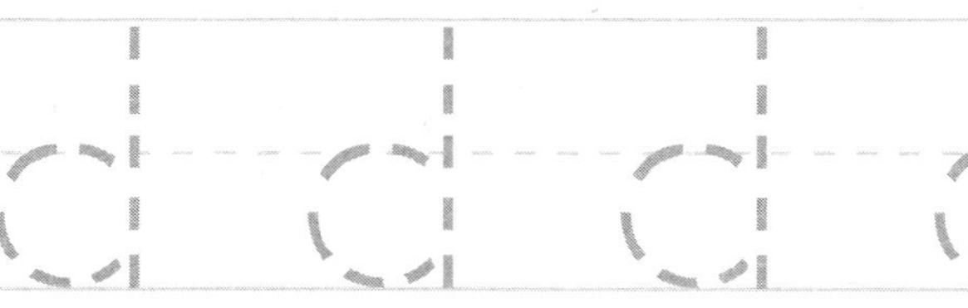

Write.

Circle each **d**.

p d b d d

Find each **d**. Color that shape yellow. Then color the rest of the picture.

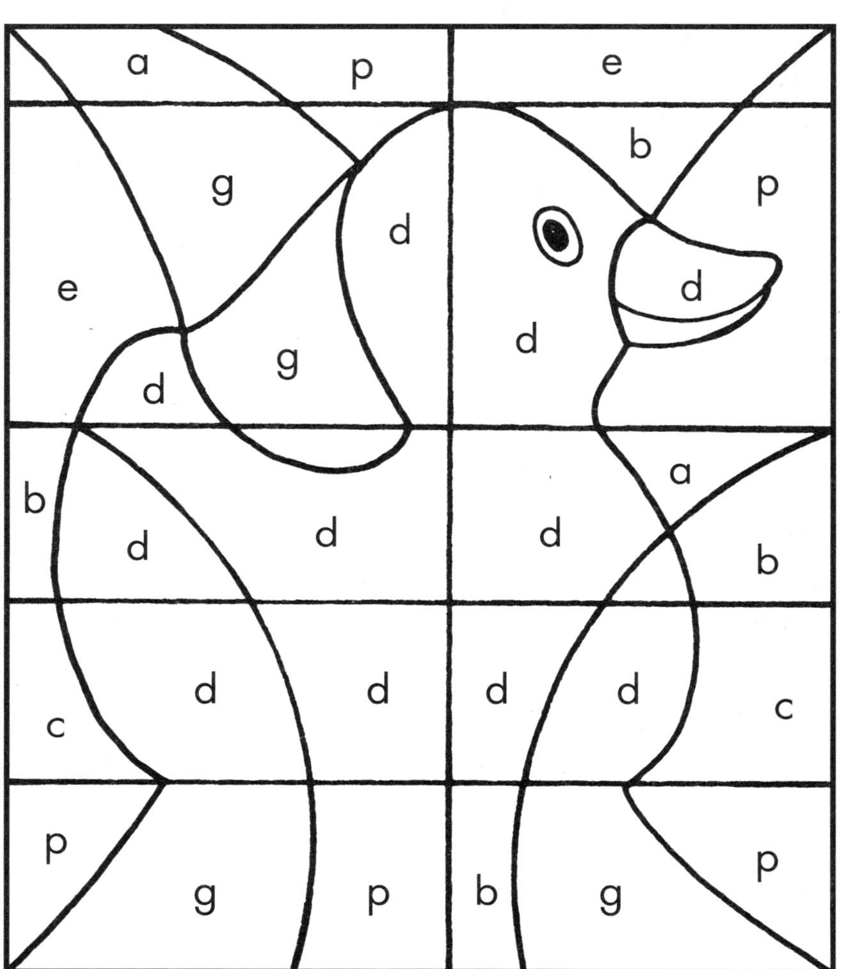

16 Name: ____________________ Lowercase d

Trace each duck. Write **d** on each one.

Trace the word below.
Read the words on the dish.
Circle each word with a **d**.

dish

17 Name: ______________________________

Trace. Write.

E E E

Find each **E**. Color that shape gray. Then color the rest of the picture.

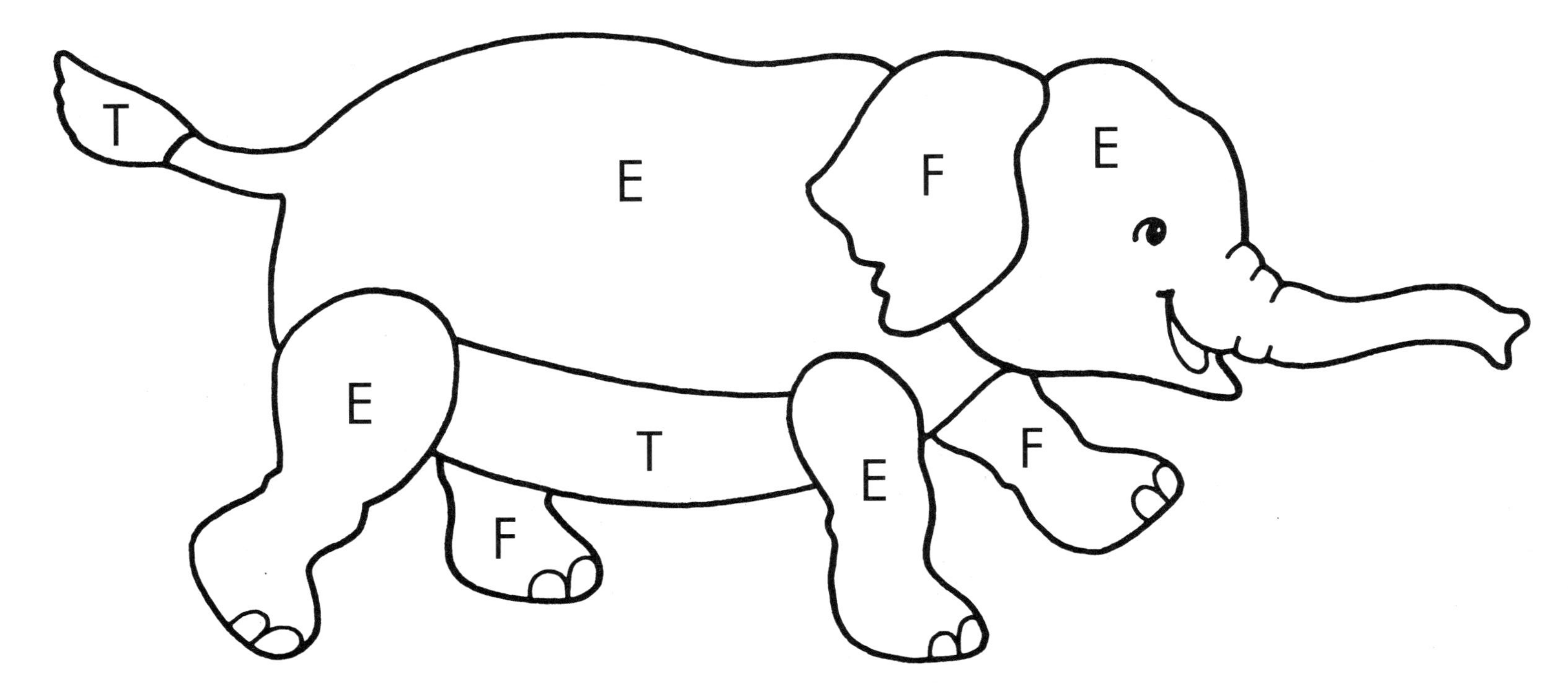

Circle each **E**.

E T E P

B E F E

Write **E** to complete the word.

_lephant

Color each item that begins with **E**.

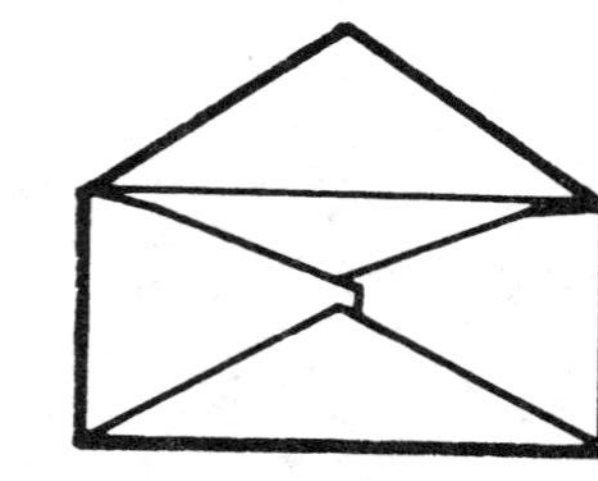

Trace.

e e e e

Write.

Circle each **e**.

e c e

e a

Find each **e**. Color that shape brown.
Then color the rest of the picture.

o p a e e c e e g d e e e r n e e e e c a p o

20 Name: ____________________ Lowercase e

Trace each egg. Write **e** on each one.

Trace the word below.
Read the words on the elephant.
Circle each word with an **e**.

elephant

cap
egg
and
end

21 Name: ______________________

Trace. Write.

Find each **F**. Color that shape orange. Then color the rest of the picture.

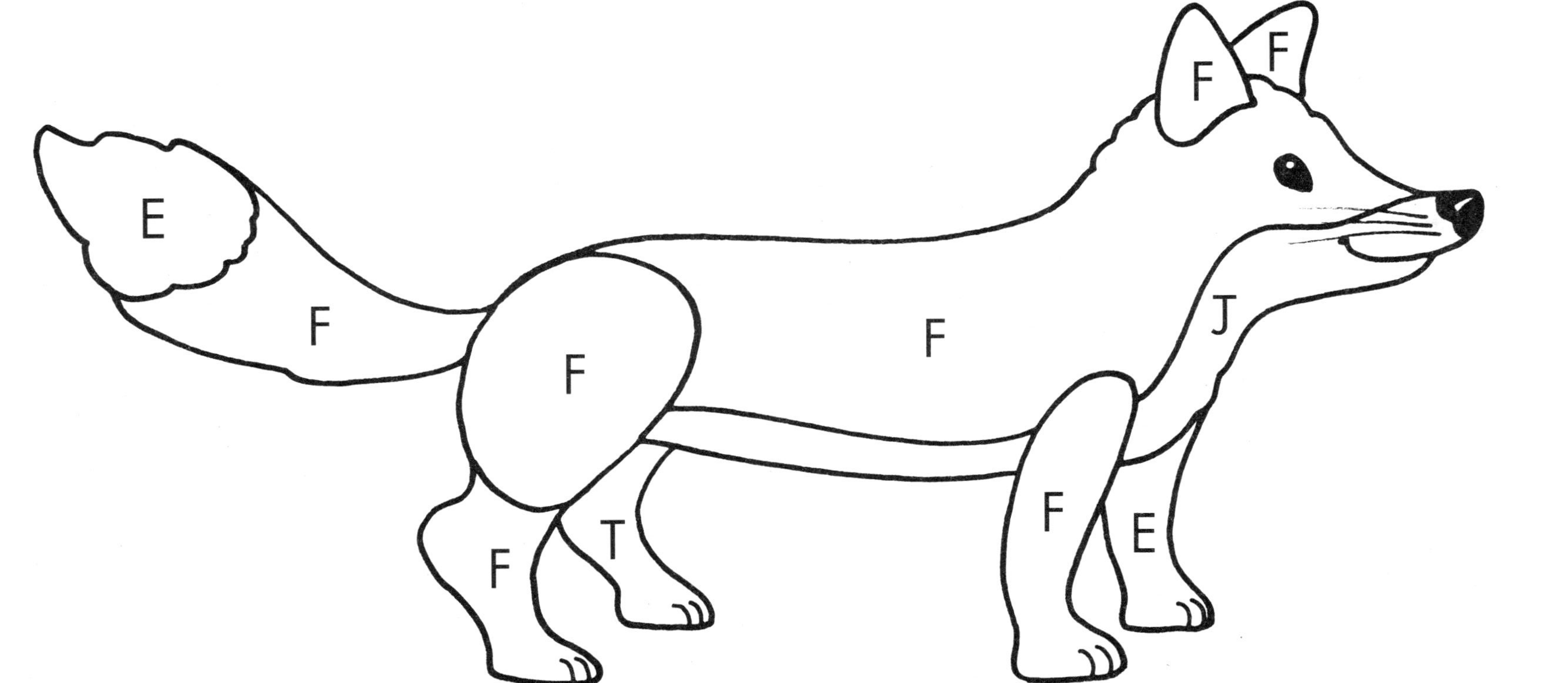

Name: ______________________

Circle each **F**.

I F E F

F B F P

Write **F** to complete the word.

ox

Color each item that begins with **F**.

Name: ______________________________

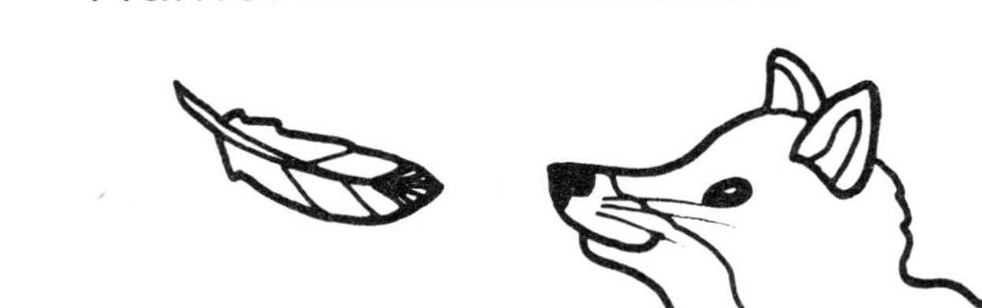

Trace.

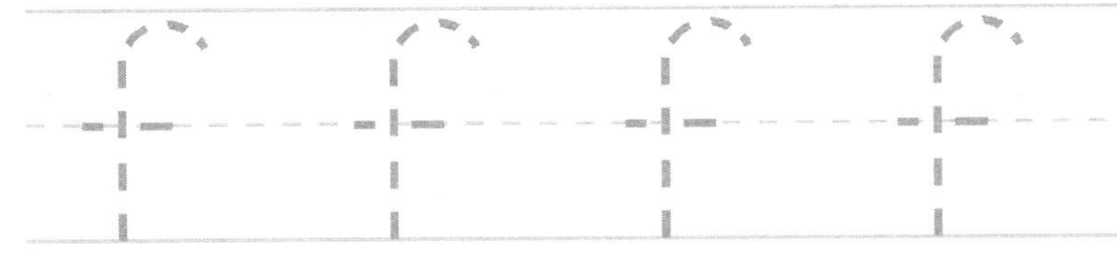

Write.

Circle each **f**.

f j f

t f

Find each **f**. Color that shape blue.
Then color the rest of the picture.

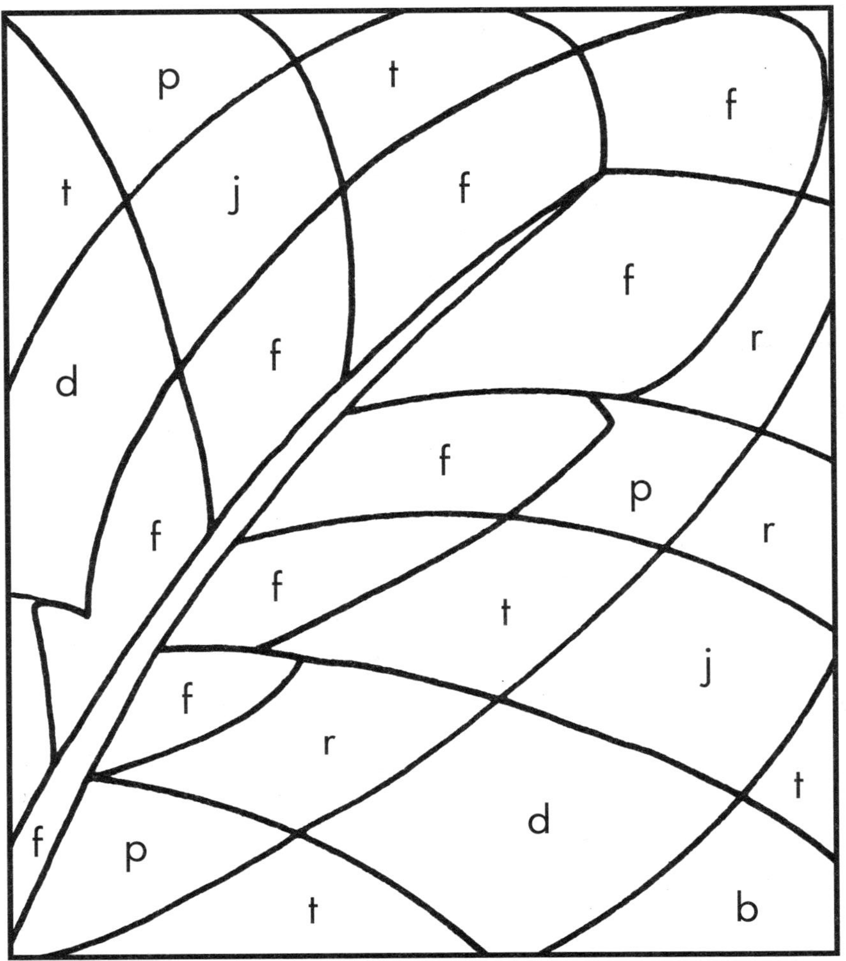

24 Name: ____________________ Lowercase f

Trace each feather. Write **f** on each one.

Trace the word below.
Read the words on the feather box.
Circle each word with an **f**.

fox

25

Name: ____________________

Trace. Write.

Find each **G**. Color that sign purple. Then color the rest of the picture.

Name: ______________________

Circle each **G**.

G O C G

G D G Q

Write **G** to complete the word.

opher

Color each item that begins with **G**.

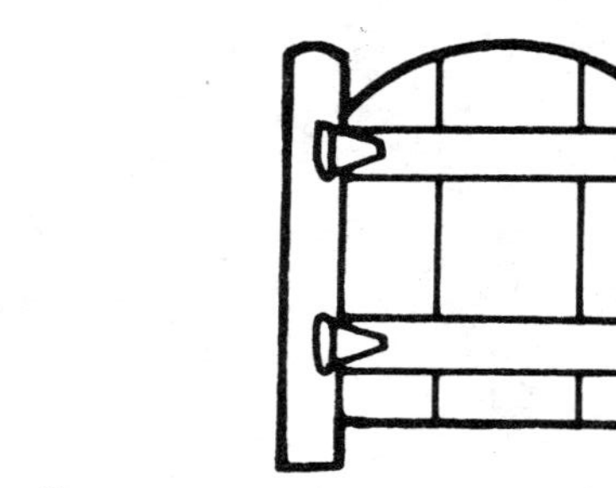
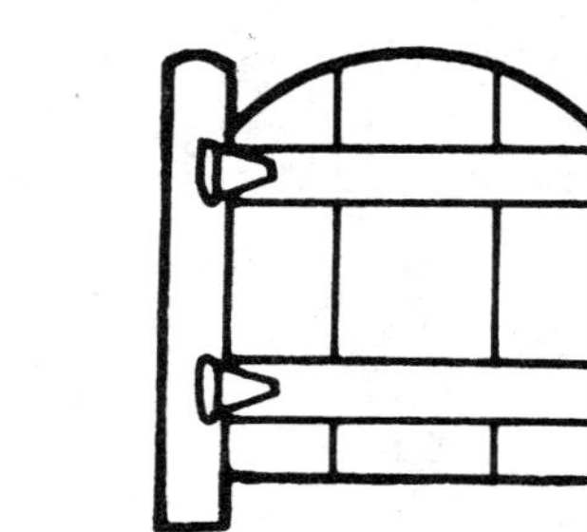

Name: ____________________

Trace.

g g g g

Write.

Circle each **g**.

g g p
g q

Find each **g**. Color that shape red.
Then color the rest of the picture.

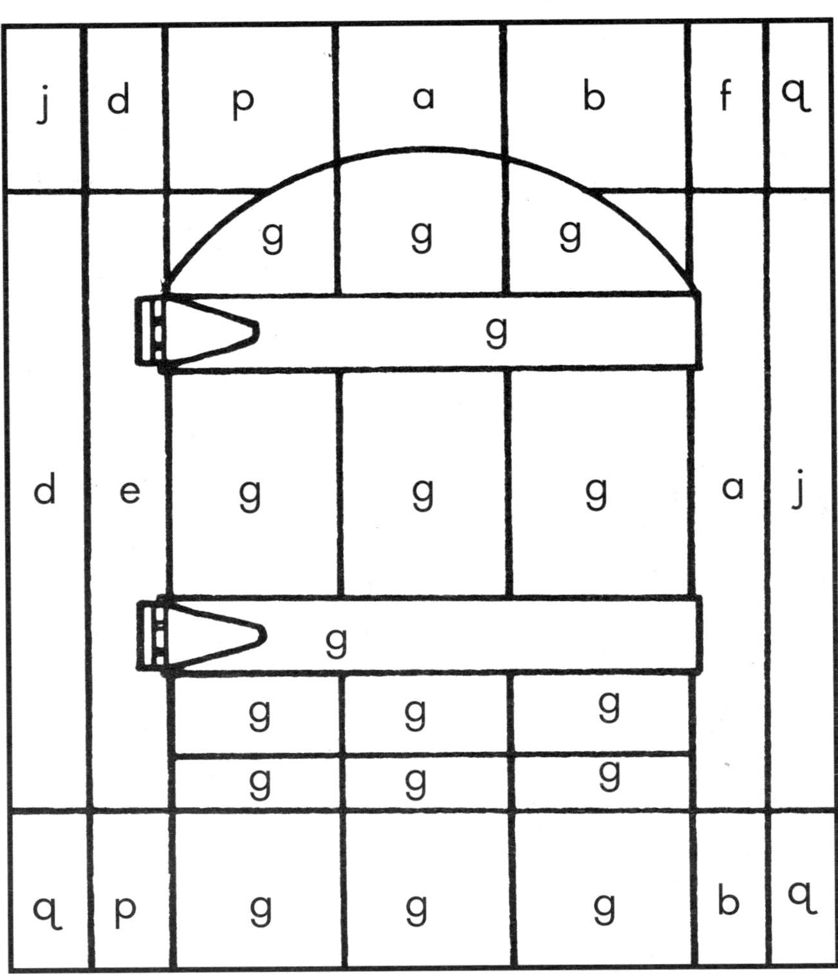

28 Name: ____________________ Lowercase g

Trace the gopher. Then write **g** on it.

Trace the word below.
Read the words on the gate.
Circle each word with a **g**.

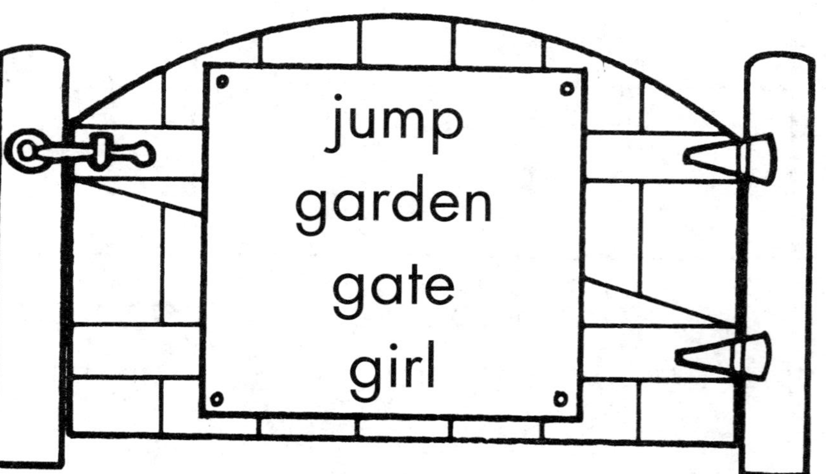

Name: ______________________

Trace. Write.

I I I

Find each **I**. Color that shape green. Then color the rest of the picture.

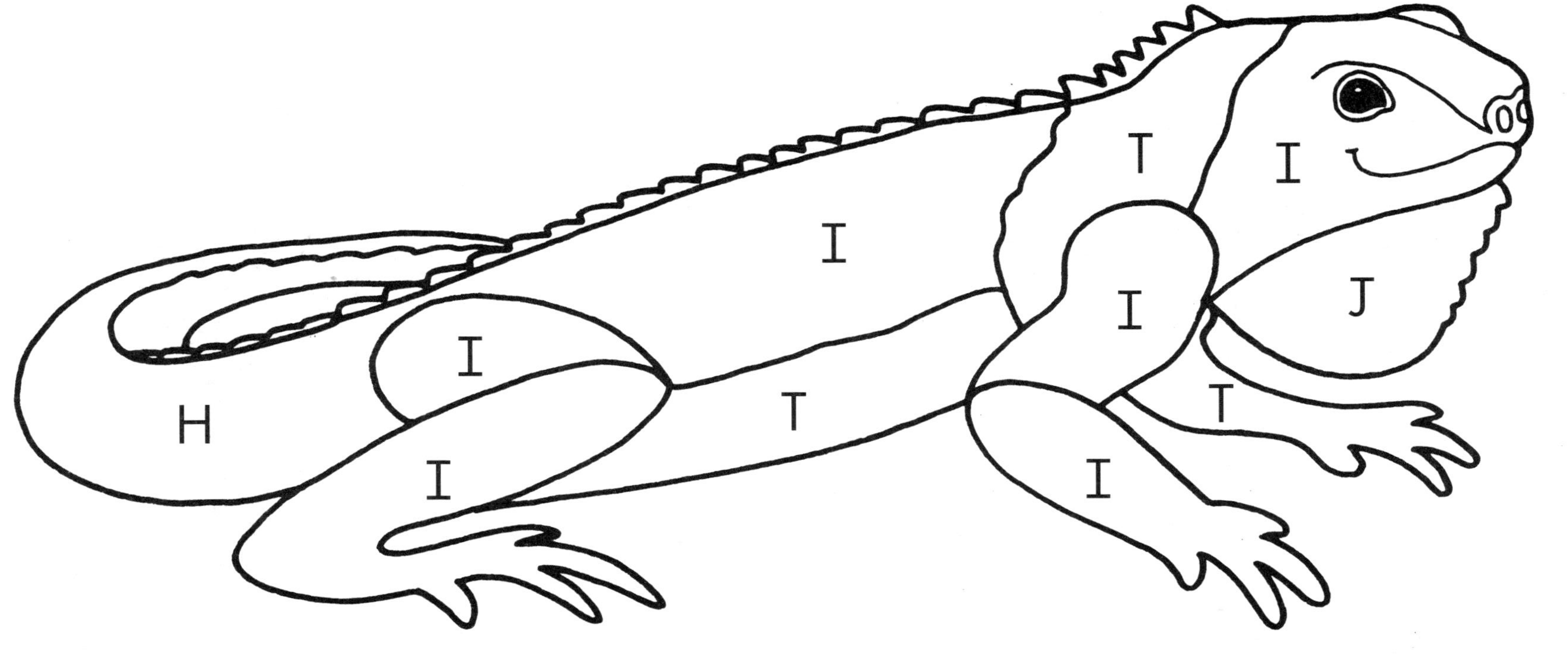

34 Name: ____________________ Uppercase I

Circle each **I**.

I M I V

H I T I

Write **I** to complete the word.

____guana

Color each item that begins with **I**.

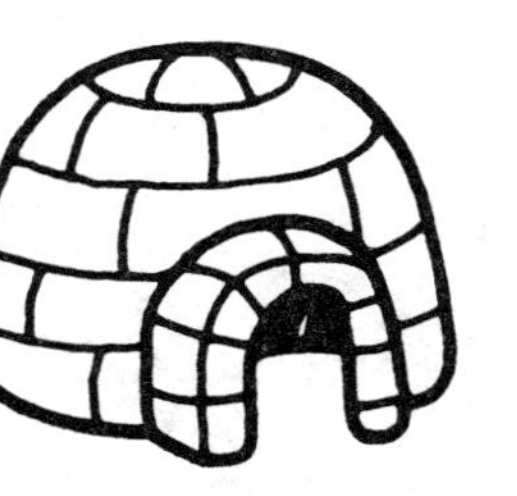

35

Name: ______________________

Trace.

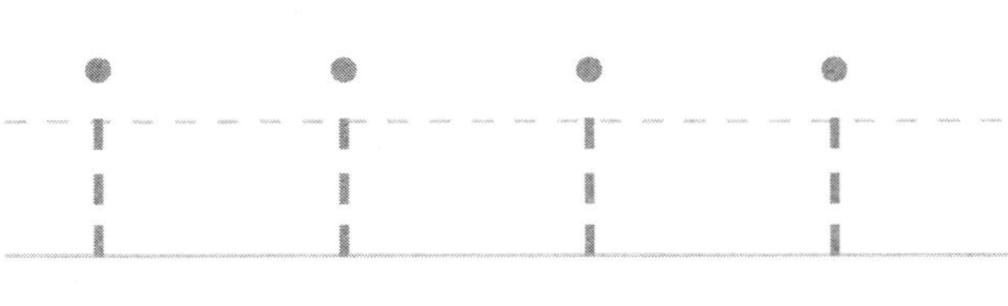

Write.

Circle each **i**.

Find each **i**. Color that shape green.
Then color the rest of the picture.

Name: ____________________

Draw insects in the jar. Write **i** on the jar lid.

Trace the word below.
Read the words on the insect jar.
Circle each word with an **i**.

insect

37 Name: ______________________

Trace. Write.

Find each **J**. Color that shape pink. Then color the rest of the picture.

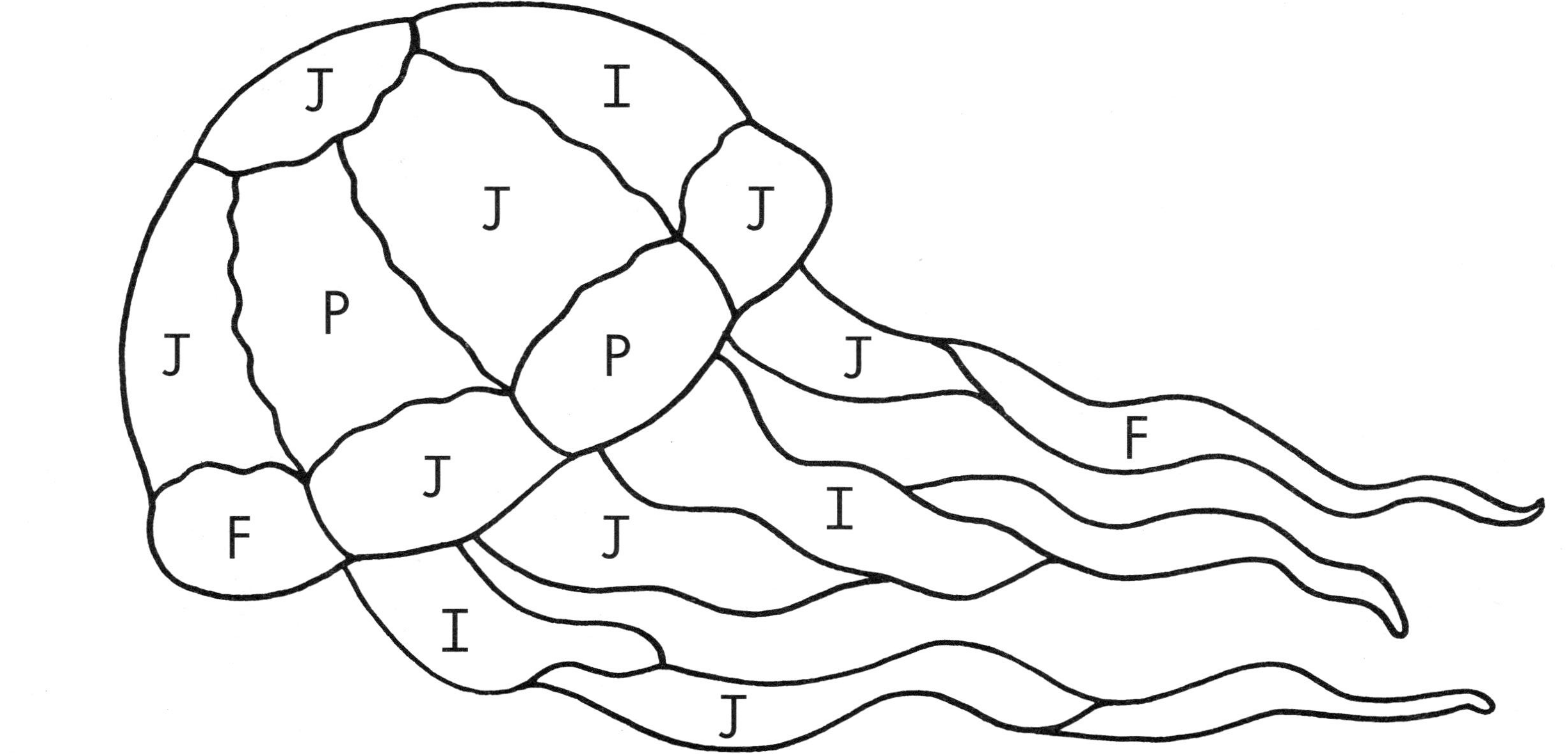

Name: ____________________

Circle each **J**.

J J F J

F G J P

Write **J** to complete the word.

ellyfish

Color each item that begins with **J**.

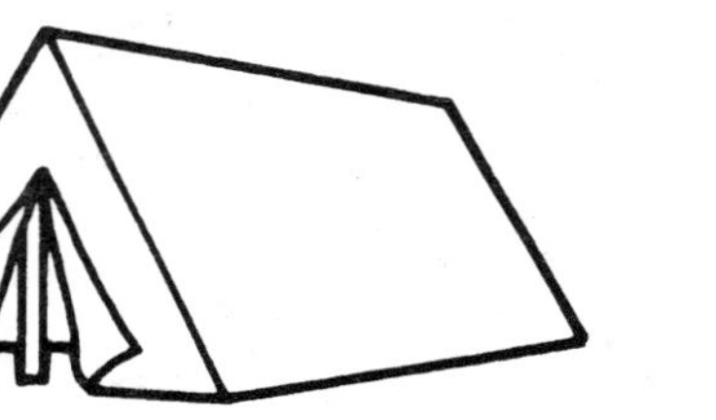

Name: ______________________

Trace.

Write.

Circle each **j**.

Find each **j**. Color that shape purple.
Then color the rest of the picture.

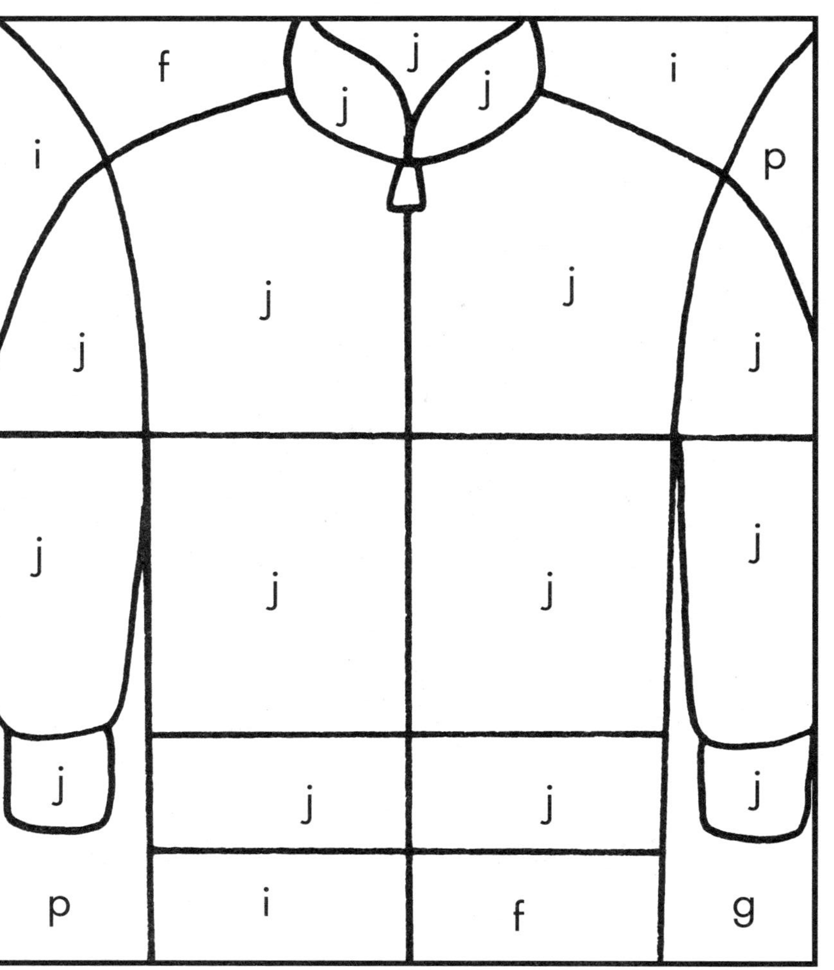

Name: ______________________

Write **j** on each jellyfish.

Trace the word below.
Read the words on the jacket.
Circle each word with a **j**.

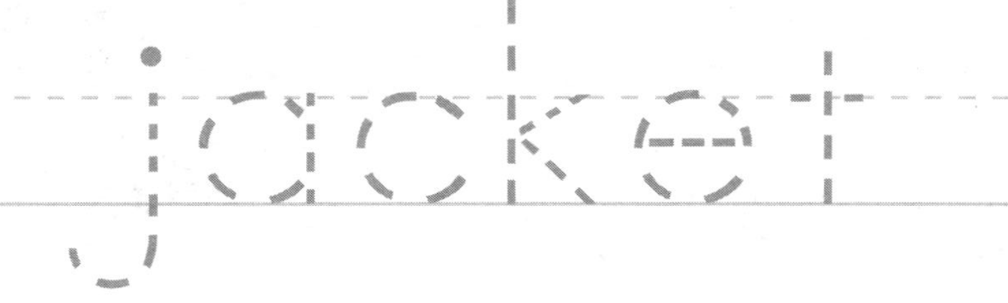

Name: ____________________

Trace. Write.

K K K

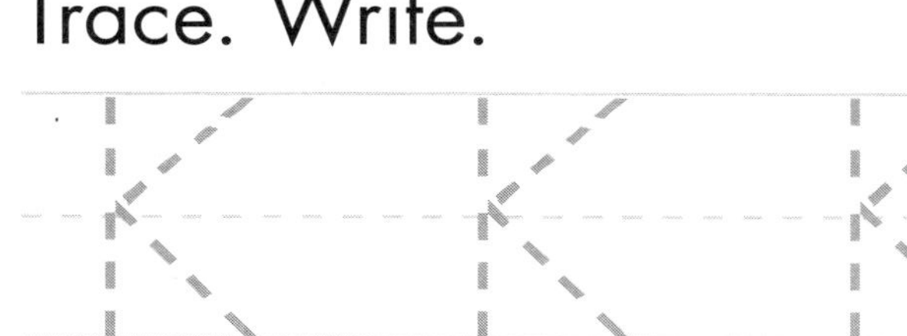

Find each **K**. Color that shape brown. Then color the rest of the picture.

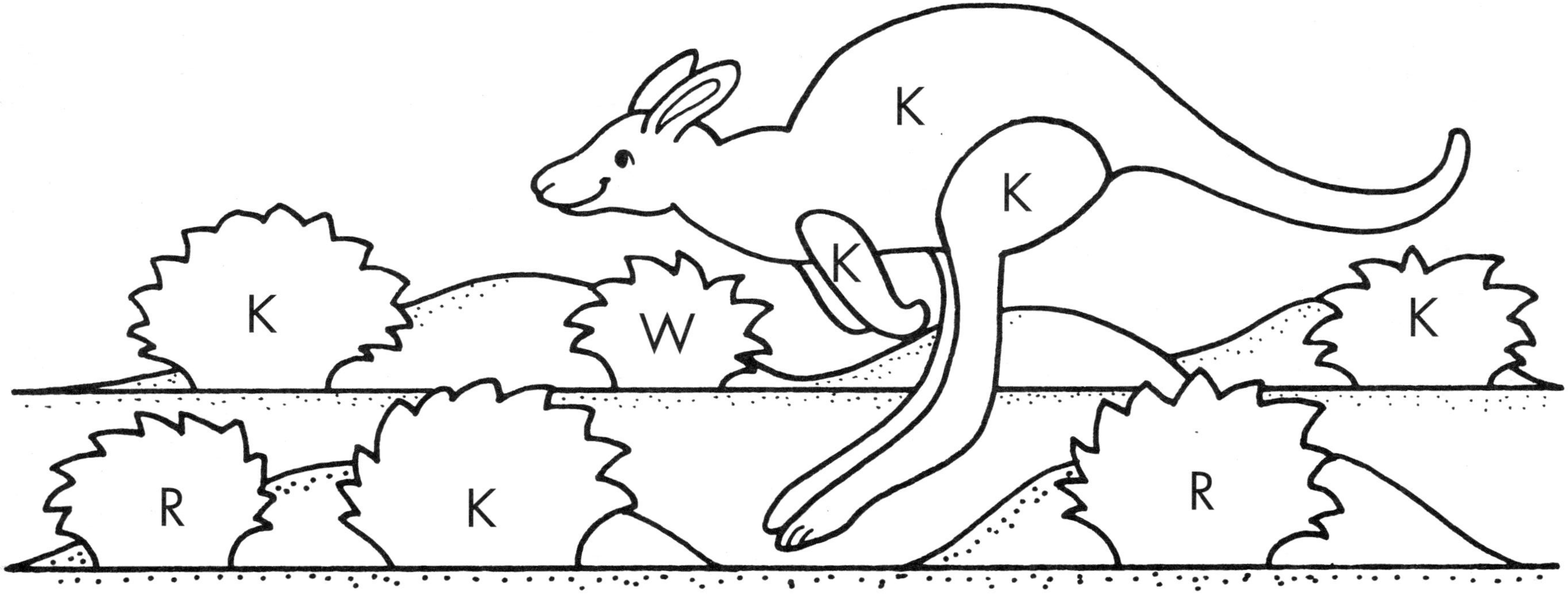

Name: ____________________

Circle each **K**.

K R K W

H K X K

Write **K** to complete the word.

___angaroo

Color each item that begins with **K**.

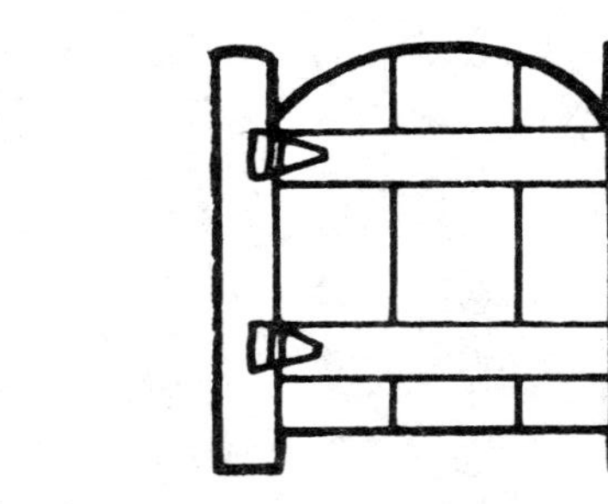
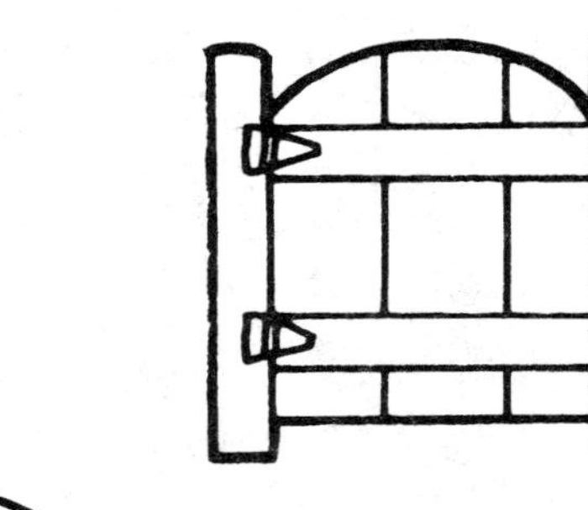

Name: ____________________

Trace.

Write.

Circle each **k**.

k v k

k l

Find each **k**. Color that shape orange.
Then color the rest of the picture.

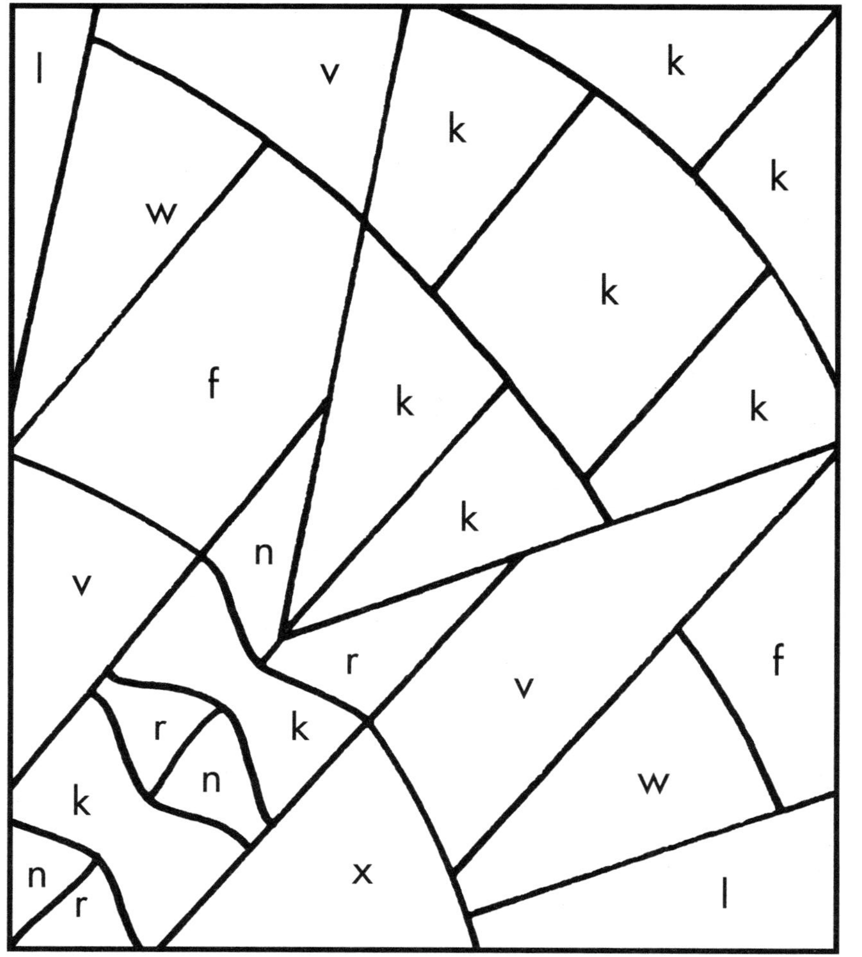

Name: ______________________

Trace the kite. Then write **k** on it.

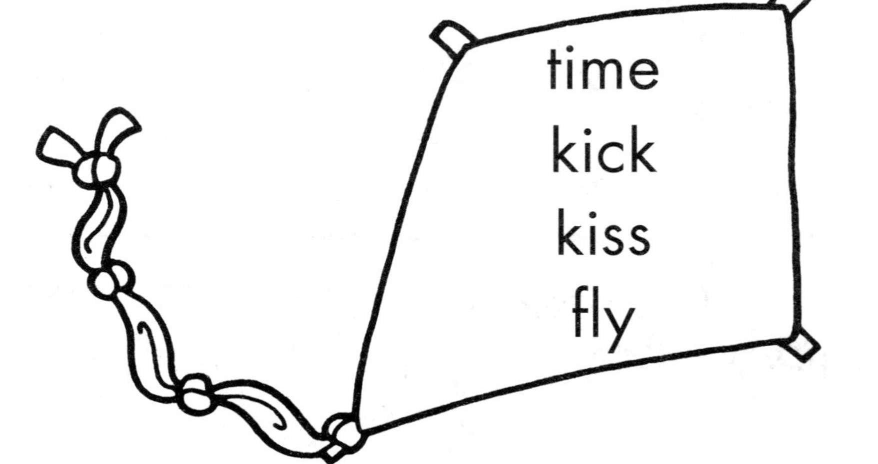

Trace the word below.
Read the words on the kite.
Circle each word with a **k**.

kite

time
kick
kiss
fly

Name: ______________________

Trace. Write.

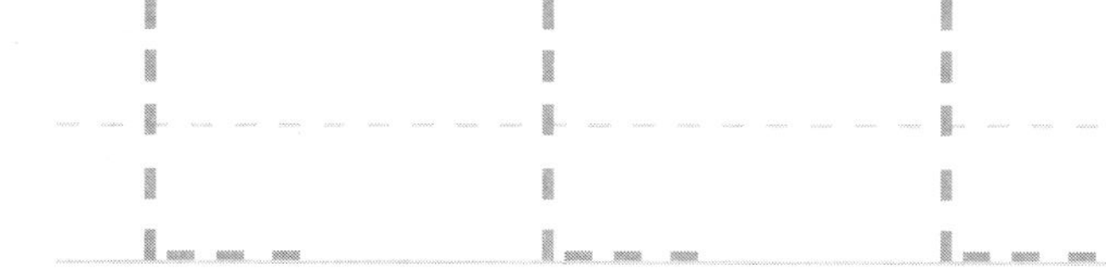

Find each **L**. Color that shape yellow. Then color the rest of the picture.

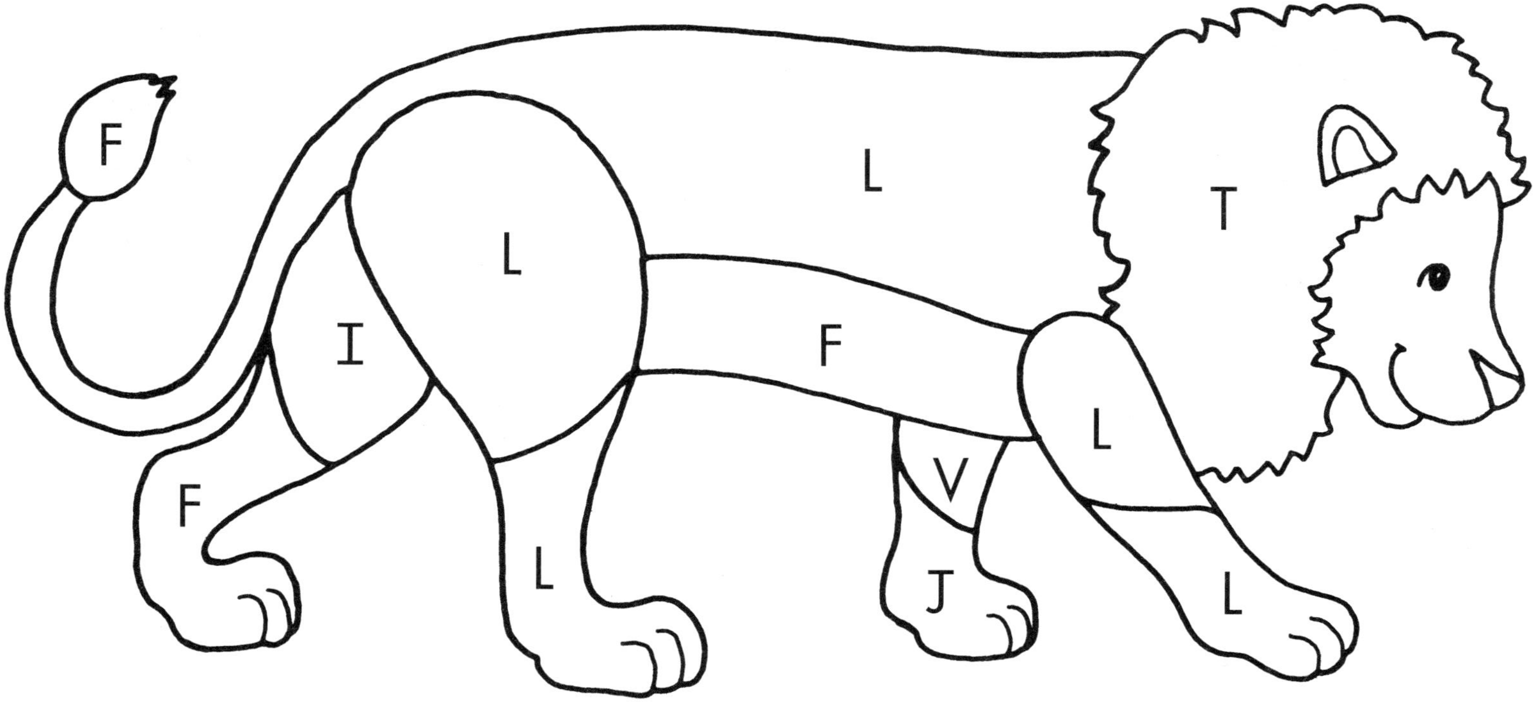

Name: ____________________

Circle each **L**.

P L E L

L J L F

Write **L** to complete the word.

___ion

Color each item that begins with **L**.

Name: ______________________

Trace.

Write.

Circle each **l**.

Find each **l**. Color that shape red.
Then color the rest of the picture.

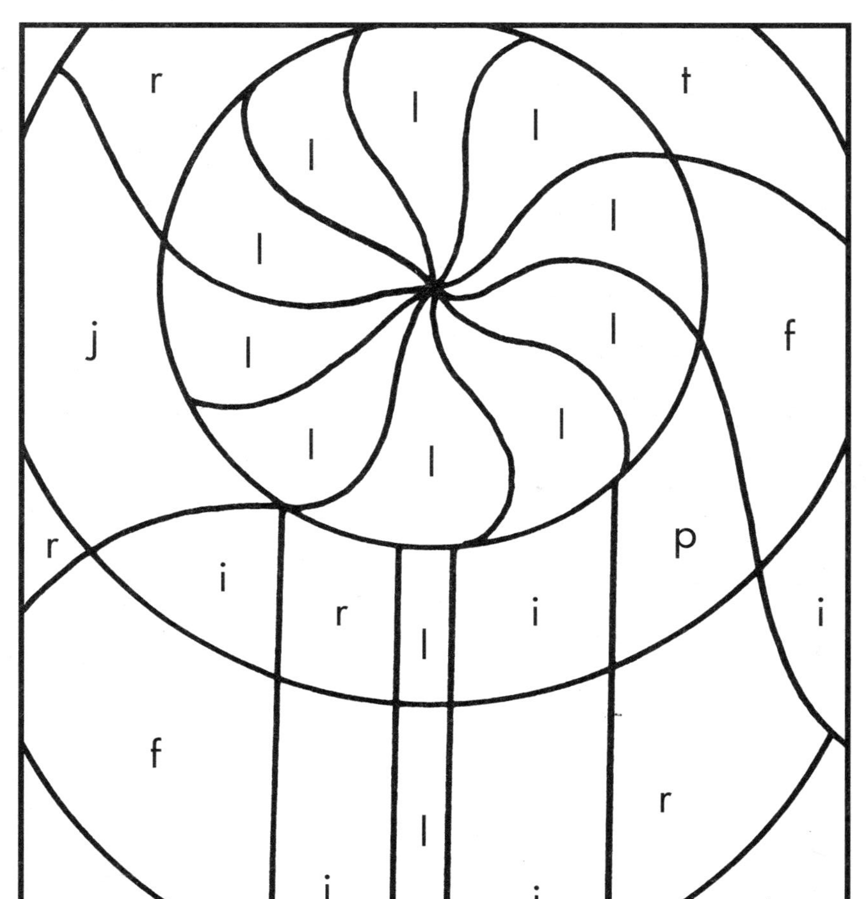

Name: ____________________

Trace each lollipop. Write **l** on each one.

Trace the word below.
Read the words on the large lollipop.
Circle each word with an **l**.

lollipop

Name: ____________________

Trace. Write.

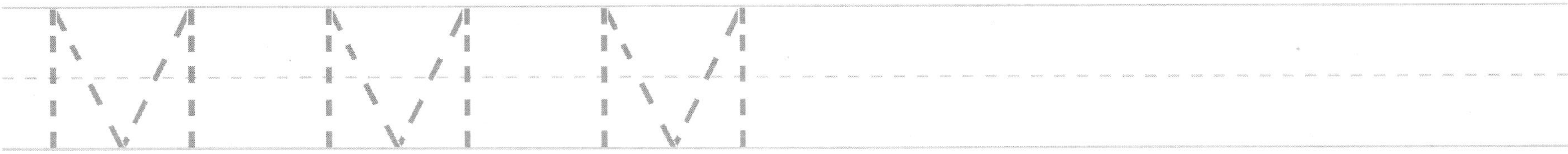

M M M

Find each **M**. Color that mitten blue. Then color the rest of the picture.

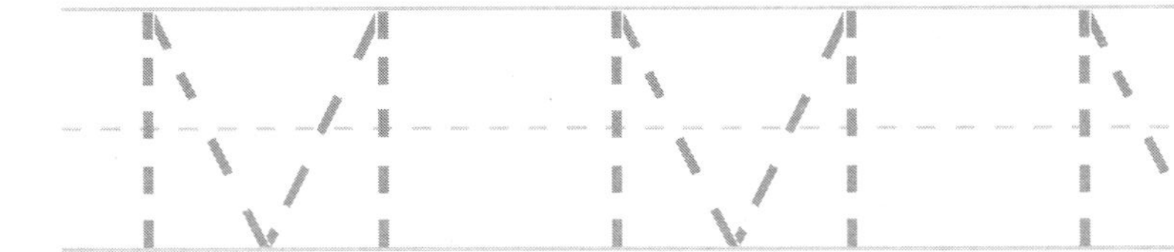

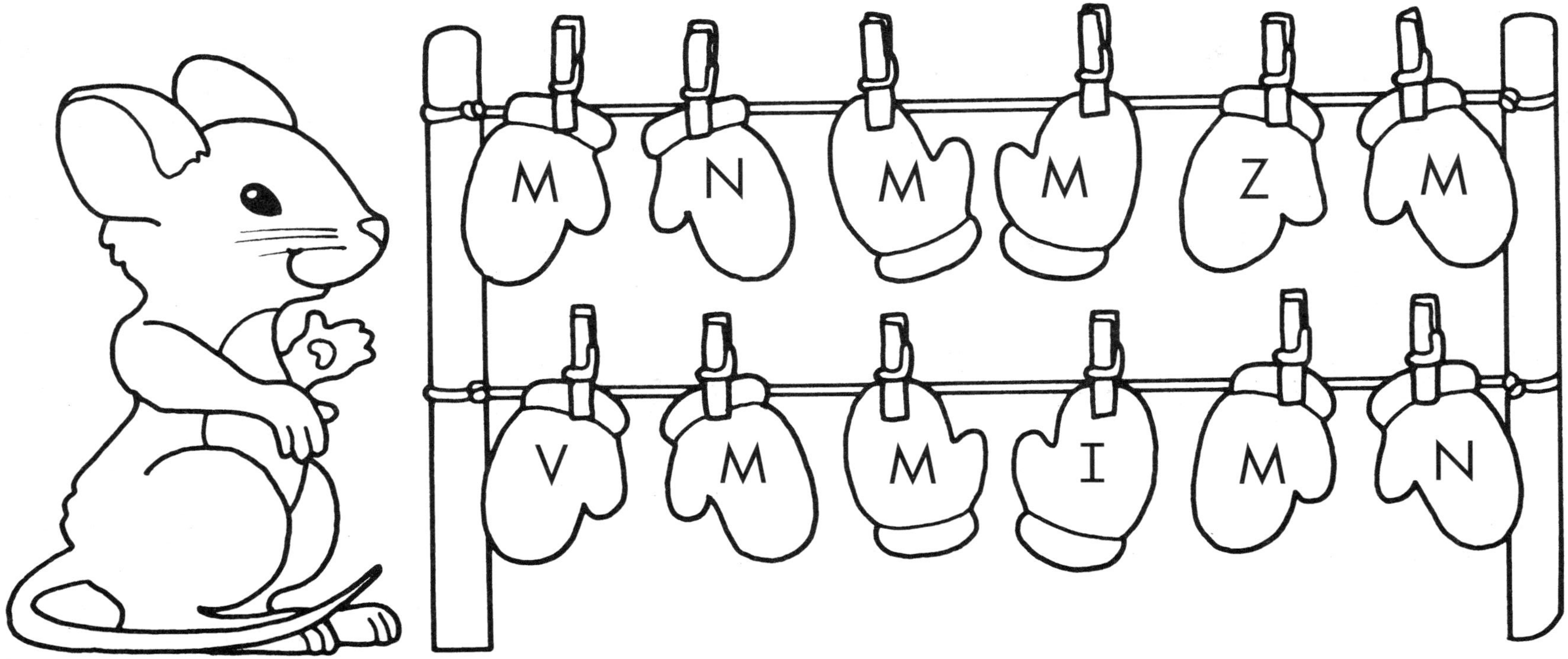

M N M M Z M

V M M I M N

 Name: ____________________

Circle each **M**.

M H N M

M Z M I

Write **M** to complete the word.

Color each item that begins with **M**.

Name: ______________________

Trace.

m m m

Write.

Circle each **m**.

w m n
m m

Find each **m**. Color that shape blue.
Then color the rest of the picture.

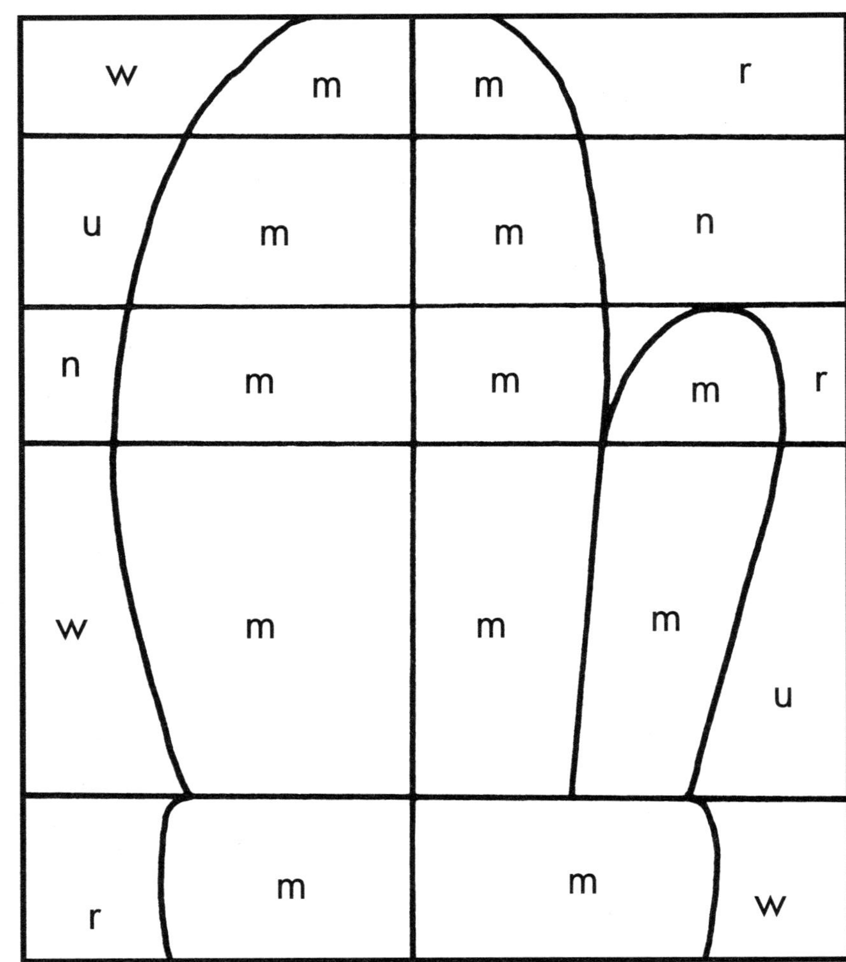

Name: ________________________________

Trace each mitten. Write **m** on each one.

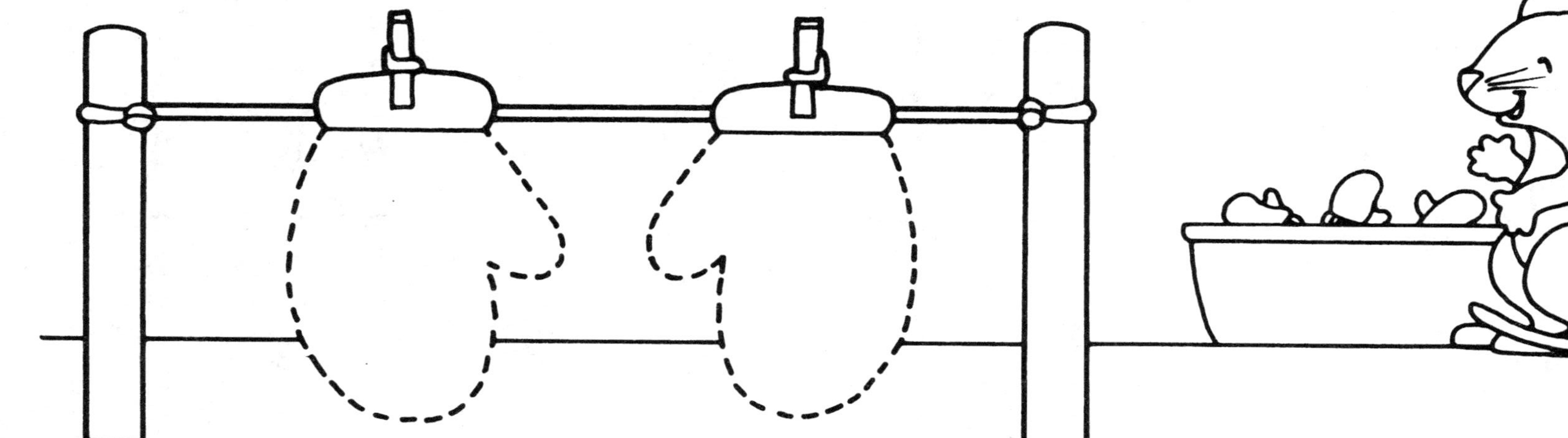

Trace the word below.
Read the words on the mitten.
Circle each word with an **m**.

mitten

Name: ______________________

Trace. Write.

N N N

Find each **N**. Color that shape brown. Then color the rest of the picture.

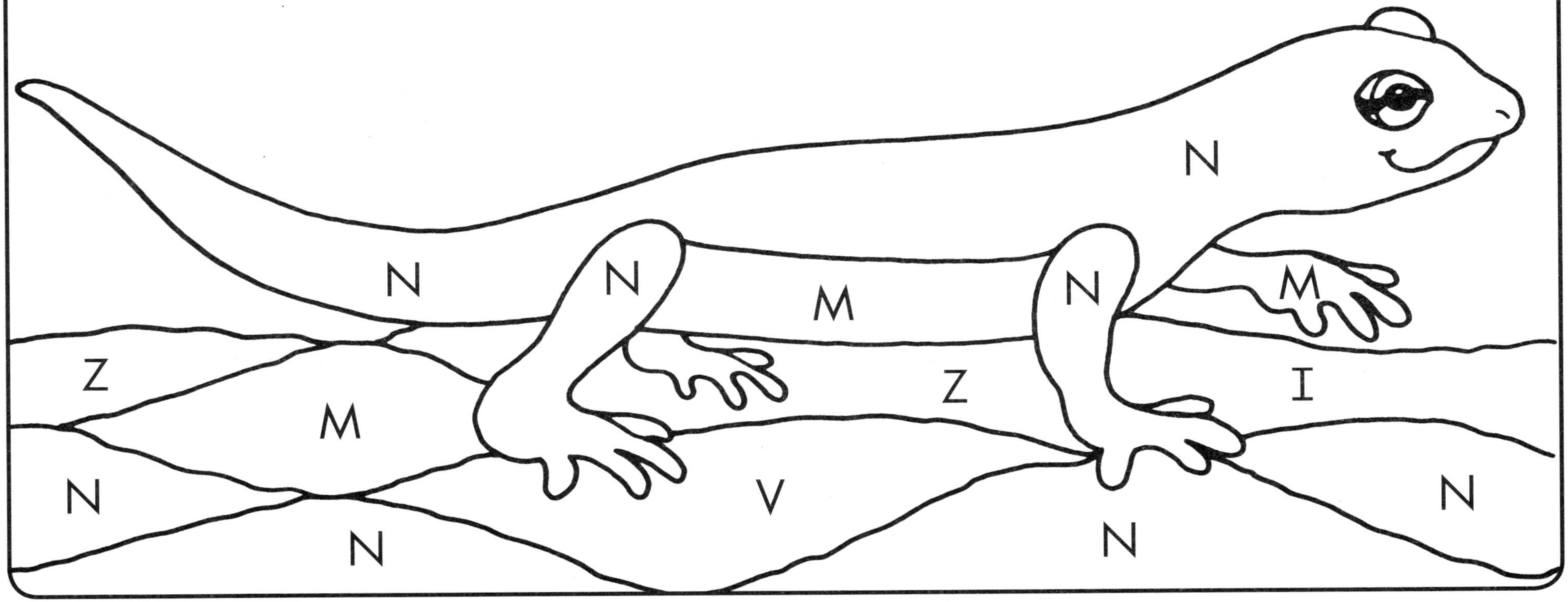

Name: ____________________

Circle each **N**.

N M N E

Z N Y N

Write **N** to complete the word.

ewt

Color each item that begins with **N**.

Trace.

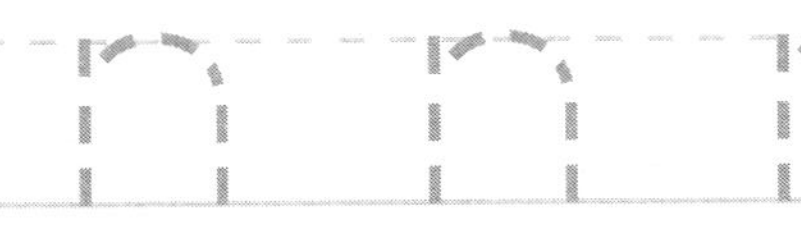

Write.

Find each **n**. Color that shape yellow. Then color the rest of the picture.

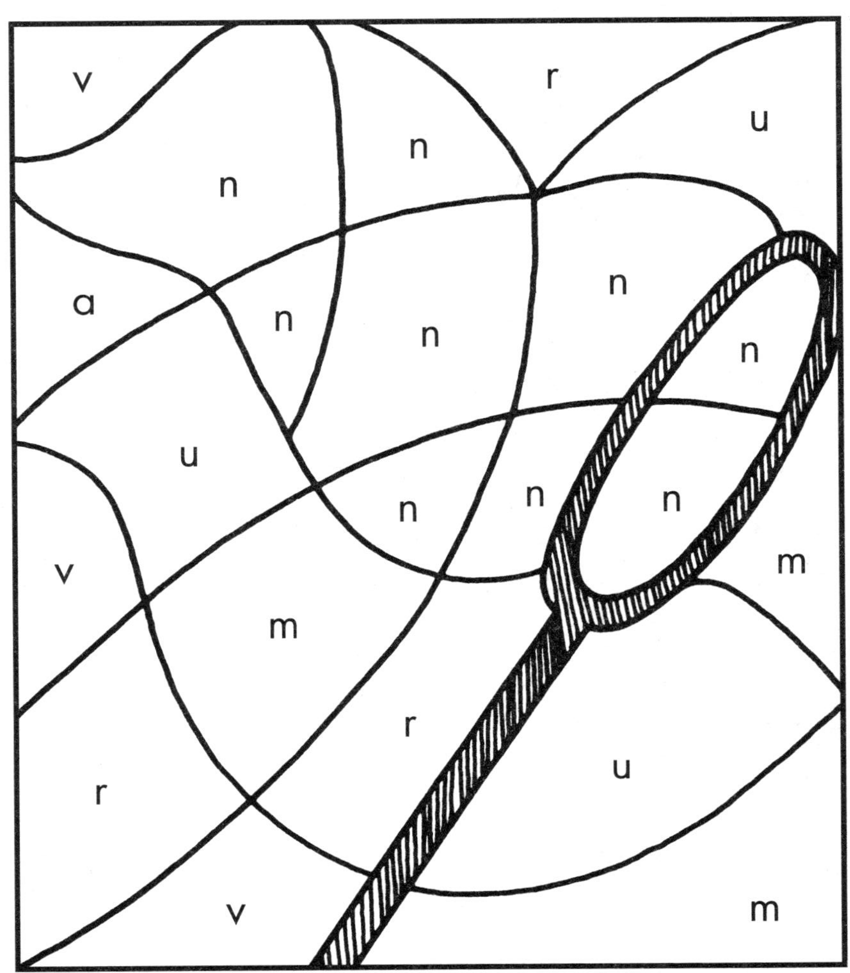

Circle each **n**.

n n m

u n

Name: ______________________

Write **n** three times on the net. Then color the newt.

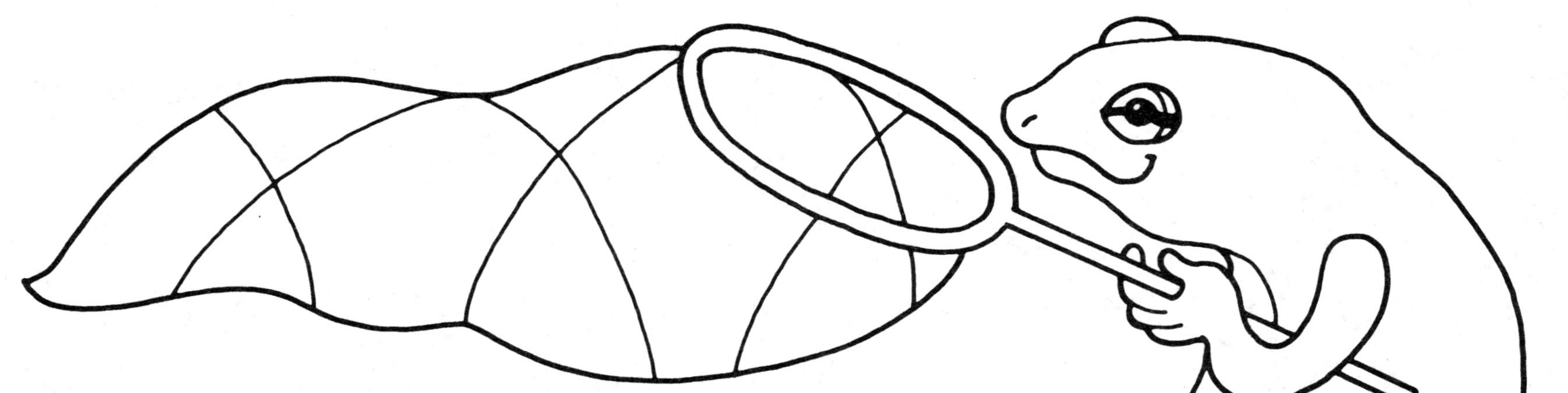

Trace the word below.
Read the words on the newt.
Circle each word with an **n**.

new
(trace)

57 Name: ____________________

Trace. Write.

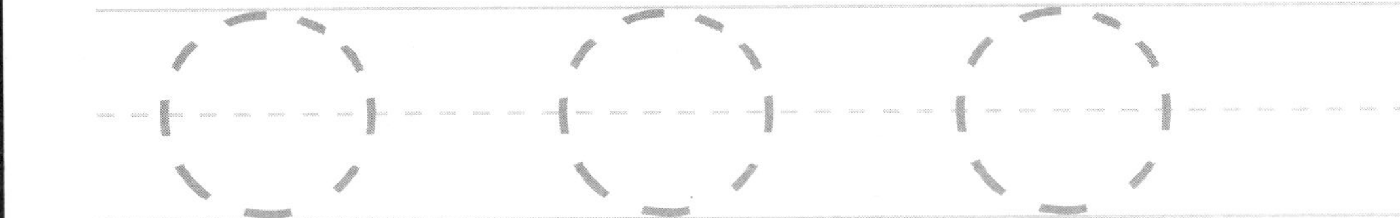

Find each **O**. Color that shape brown. Then color the rest of the picture.

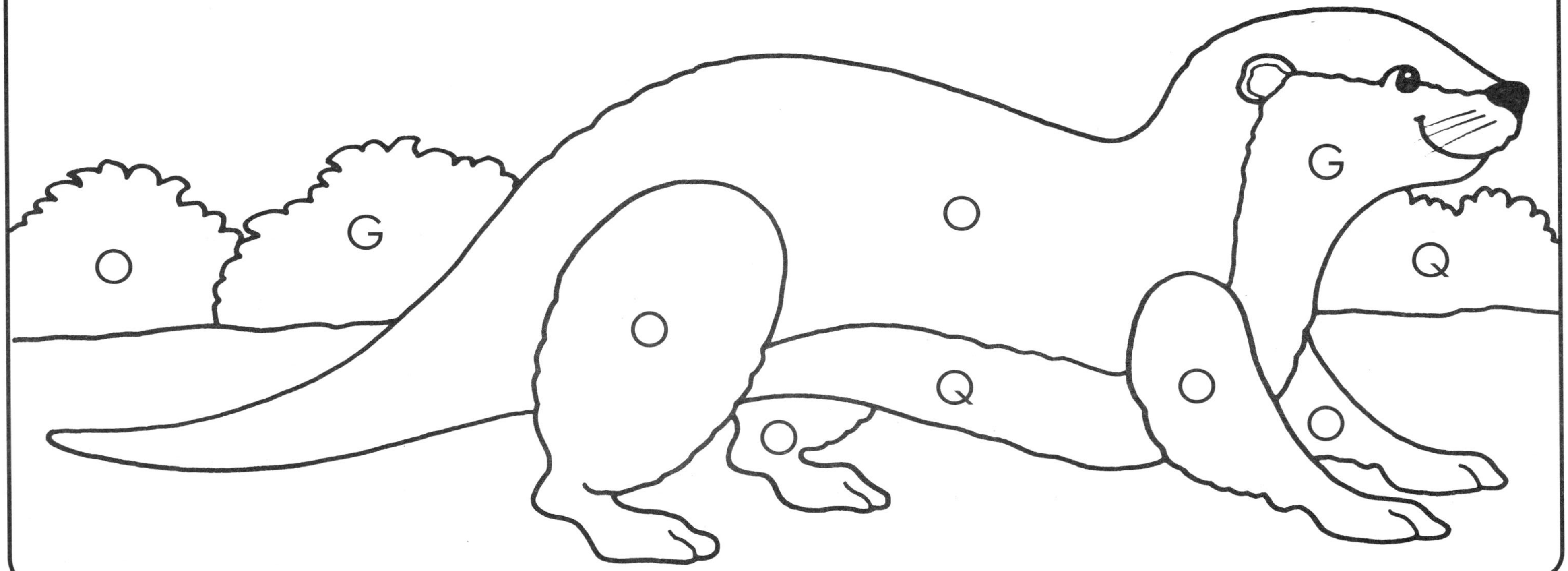

Name: ____________________

Uppercase O

Circle each O.

O Q O C

C O G O

Write O to complete the word.

tter

Color each item that begins with O.

Trace.

Write.

Circle each **o**.

o a o
c o

Find each **o**. Color that shape green. Then color the rest of the picture.

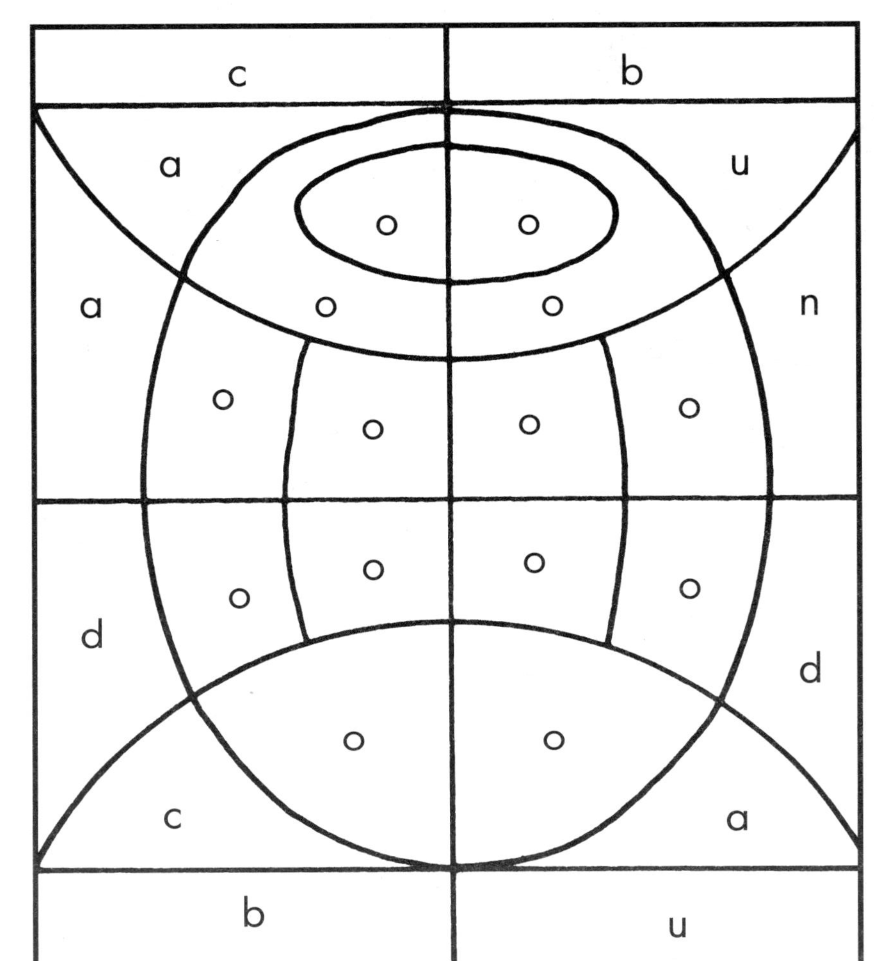

Name: ______________________

Trace each olive. Write **o** on each one.

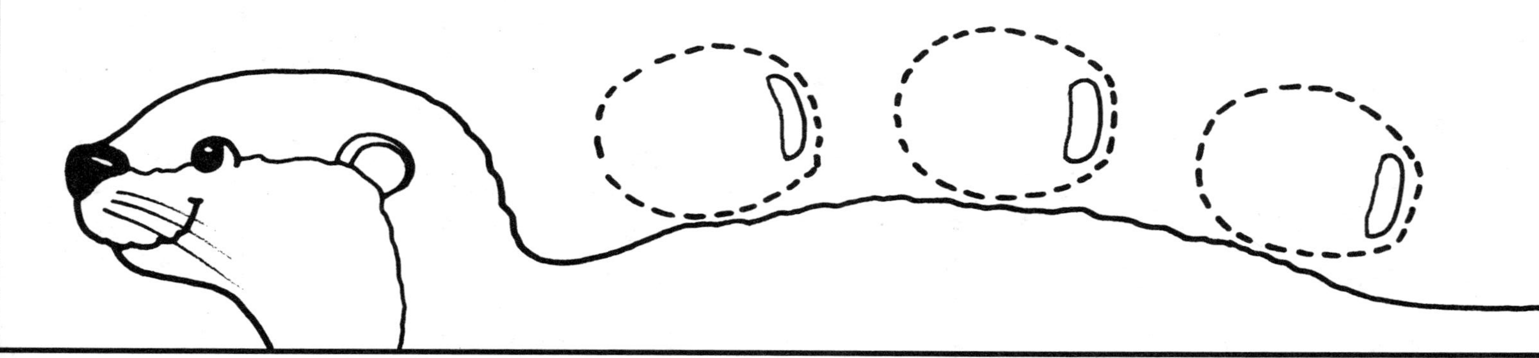

Trace the word below.
Read the words on the olive can.
Circle each word with an **o**.

olives

Name: ____________________

Trace. Write.

P P P

Find each **P**. Color that shape pink. Then color the rest of the picture.

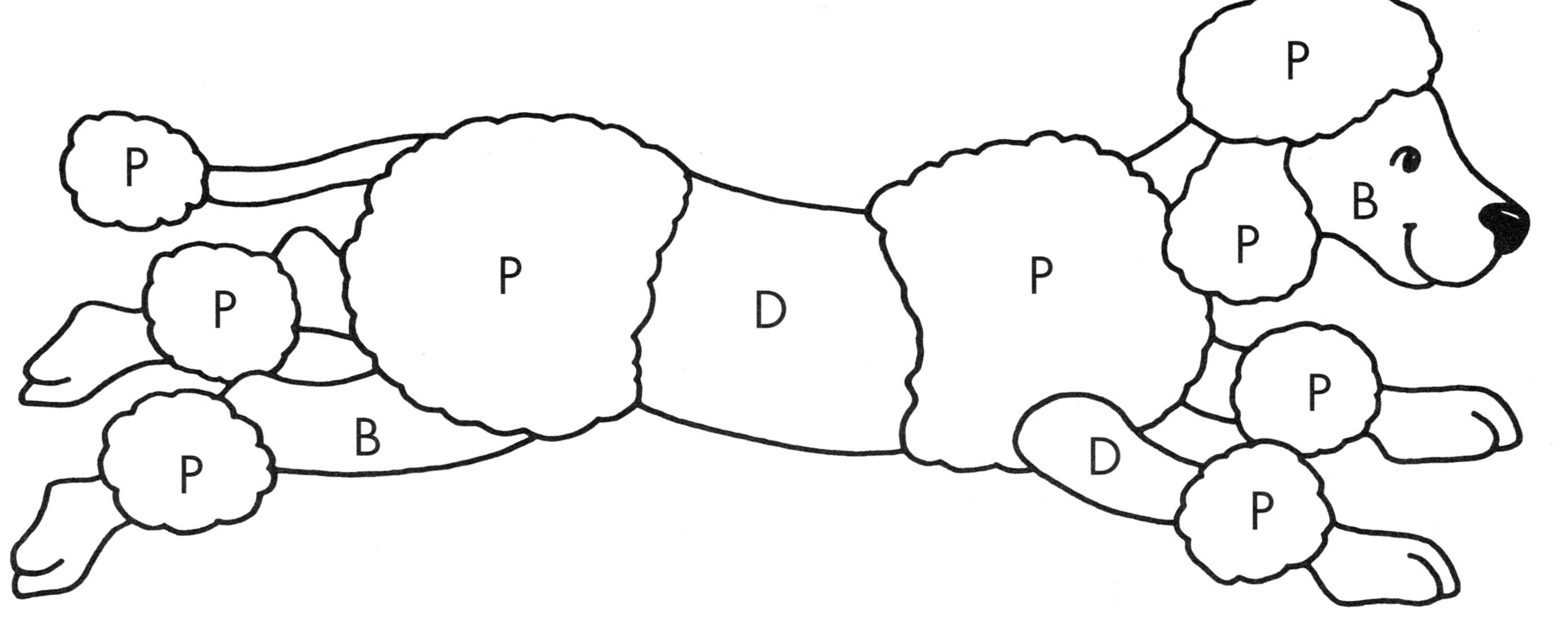

Name: ______________________

Circle each **P**.

P P B P

B U P D

Write **P** to complete the word.

_oodle

Color each item that begins with **P**.

 Name: ______________________

Trace.

p p p p

Write.

Find each **p**. Color that shape pink. Then color the rest of the picture.

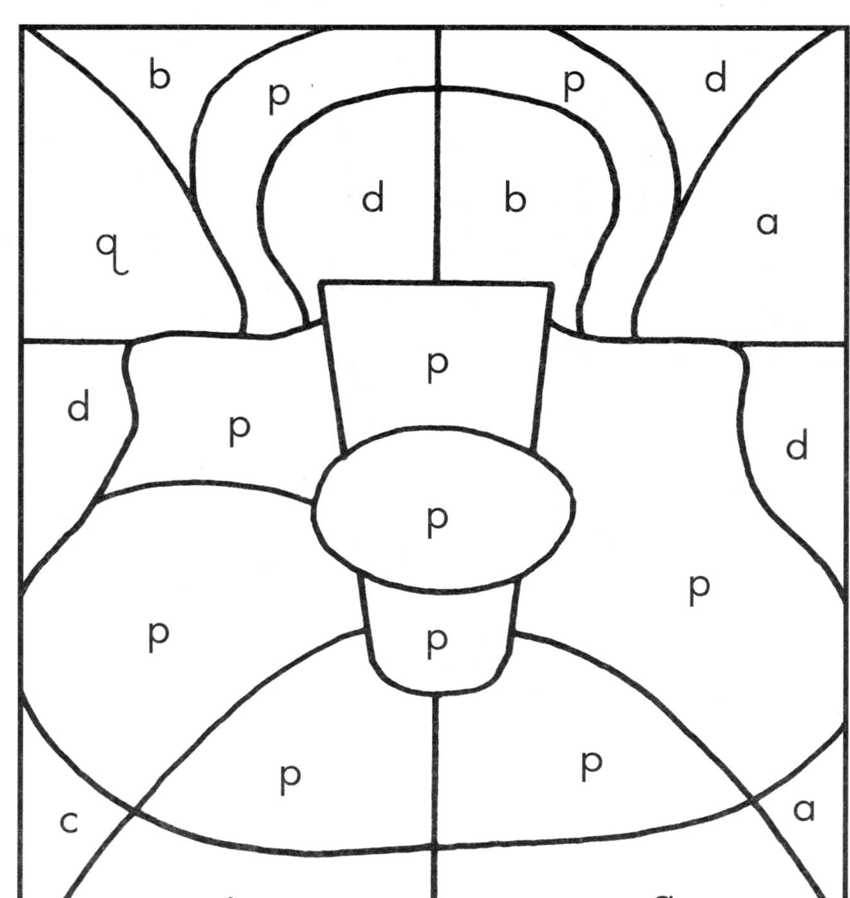

Circle each **p**.

p b p
p d

Name: ____________________

Trace each purse. Write **p** on each one.

Trace the word below.
Read the words on the purse.
Circle each word with a **p**.

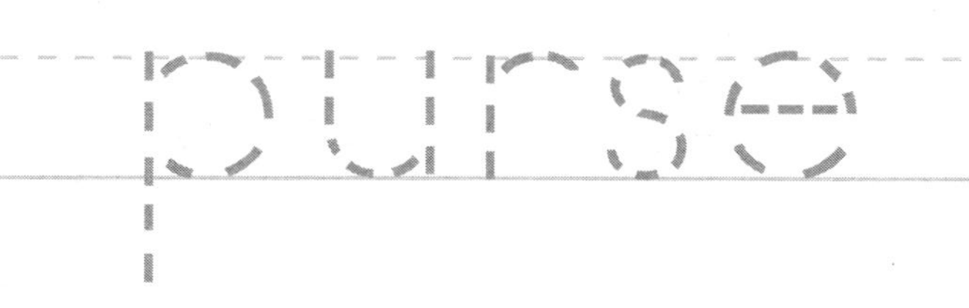

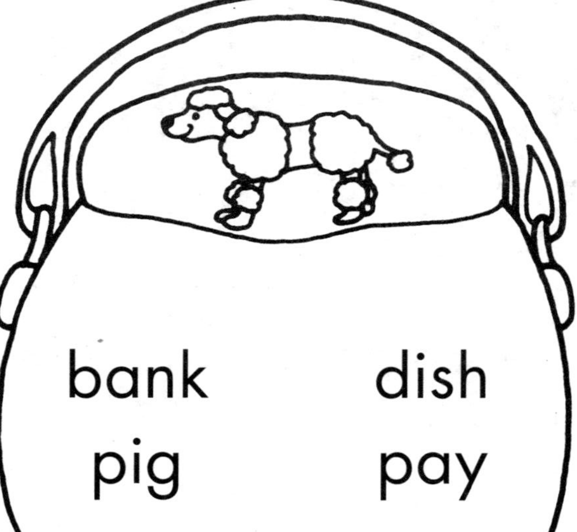

65 Name: ____________________ Uppercase Q

Trace. Write.

Find each **Q**. Color that shape brown. Then color the rest of the picture.

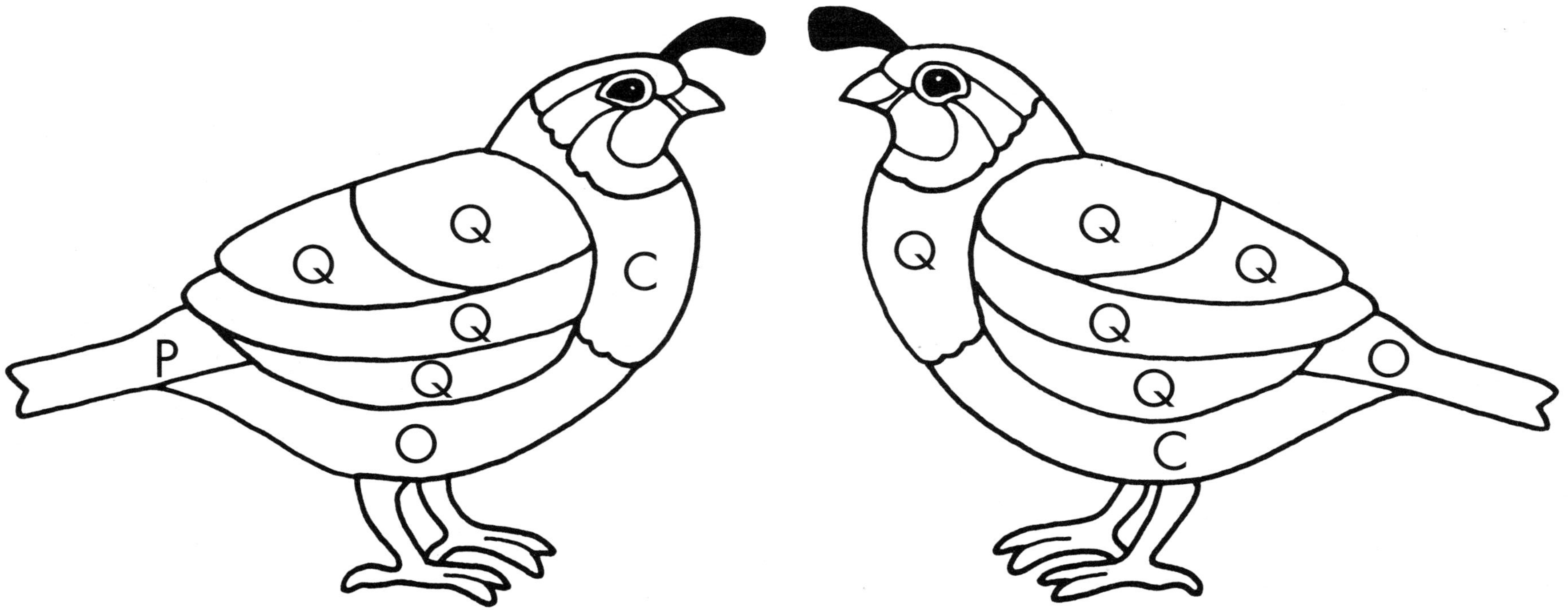

Name: ____________________

Circle each **Q**.

Q C Q O

O Q D Q

Write **Q** to complete the word.

uail

Color each item that begins with **Q**.

Name: ____________________

Trace.

q q q q

Write.

Circle each **q**.

q p q
q b

Find each **q**. Color that shape orange.
Then color the rest of the picture.

g p a c
q q q
q q q d
a q q q p
d q q q
c g

Name: ____________________

Write **q** on each large quilt square. Then color the quilt.

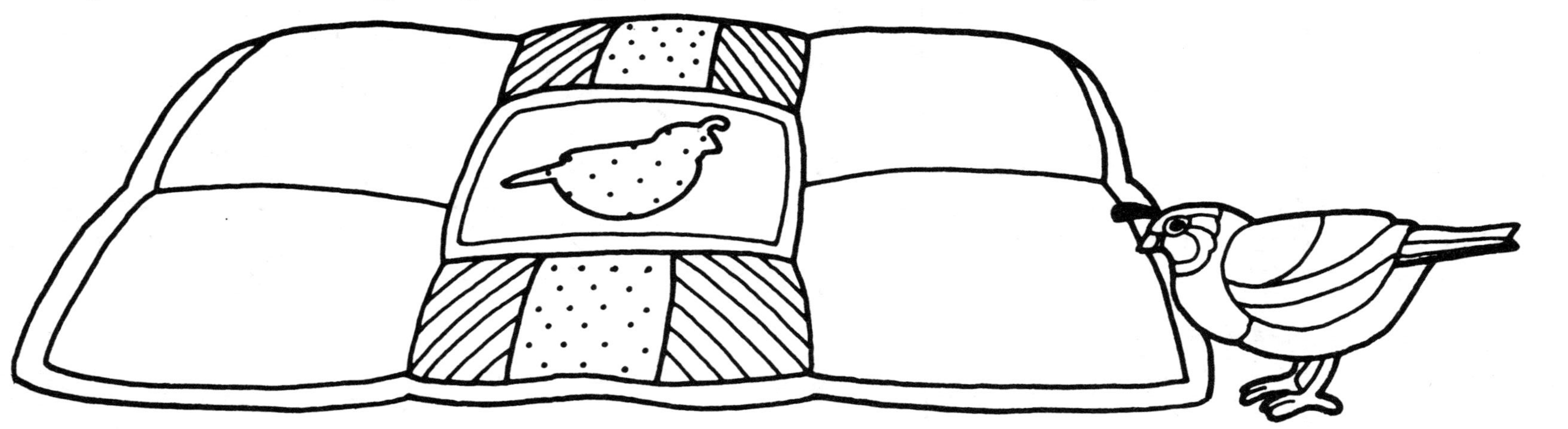

Trace the word below.
Read the words on the quilt.
Circle each word with a **q**.

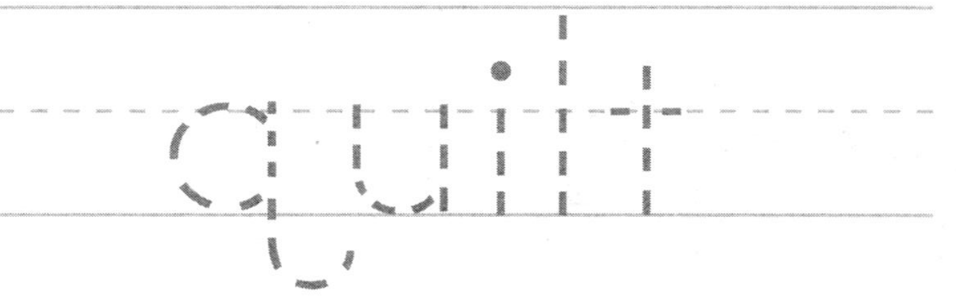

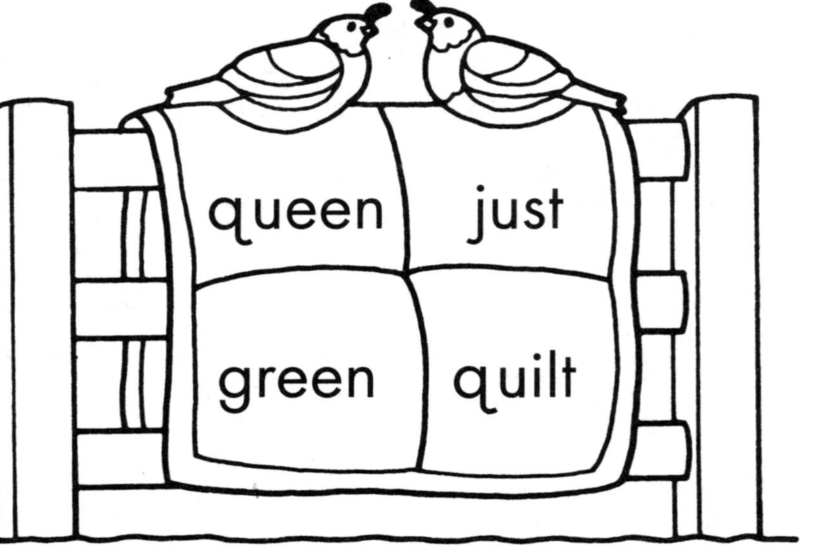

69 Name: ____________________

Trace. Write.

R R R

Find each **R**. Color that shape gray. Then color the rest of the picture.

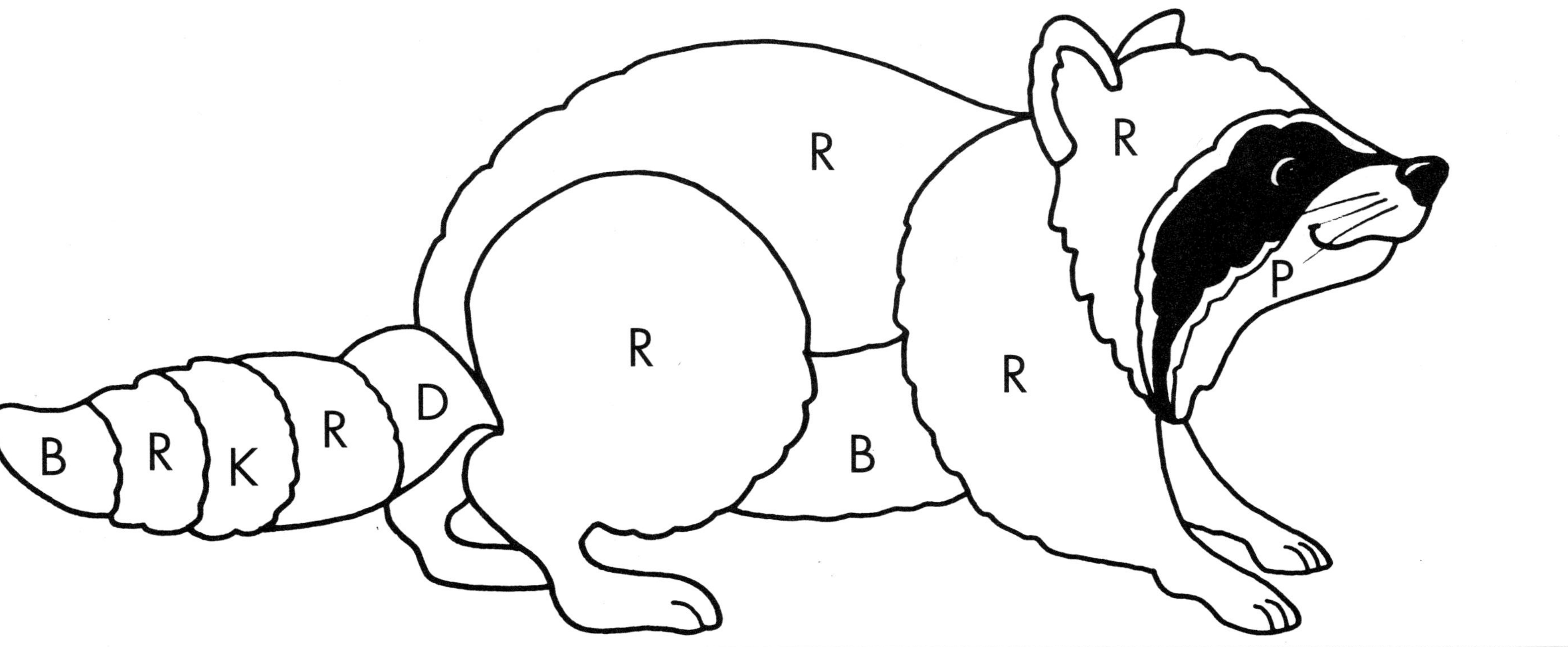

Name: ____________________

Circle each **R**.

B R K R

R P R B

Write **R** to complete the word.

_accoon

Color each item that begins with **R**.

Name: ______________________

Trace.

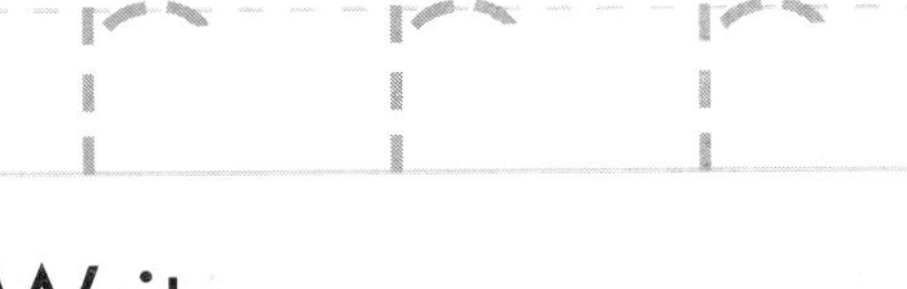

Write.

Circle each **r**.

r n r

u r

Find each **r**. Color that shape red. Then color the rest of the picture.

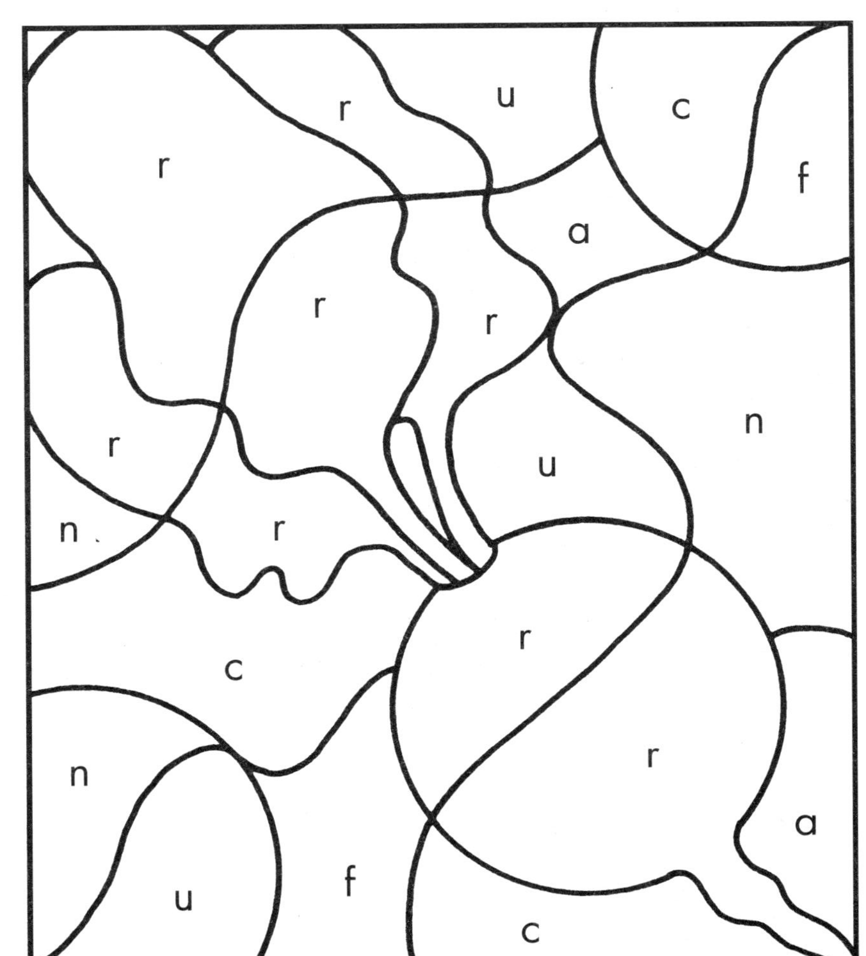

Trace each radish. Write **r** on each one.

Trace the word below.
Read the words on the radishes.
Circle each word with an **r**.

radish

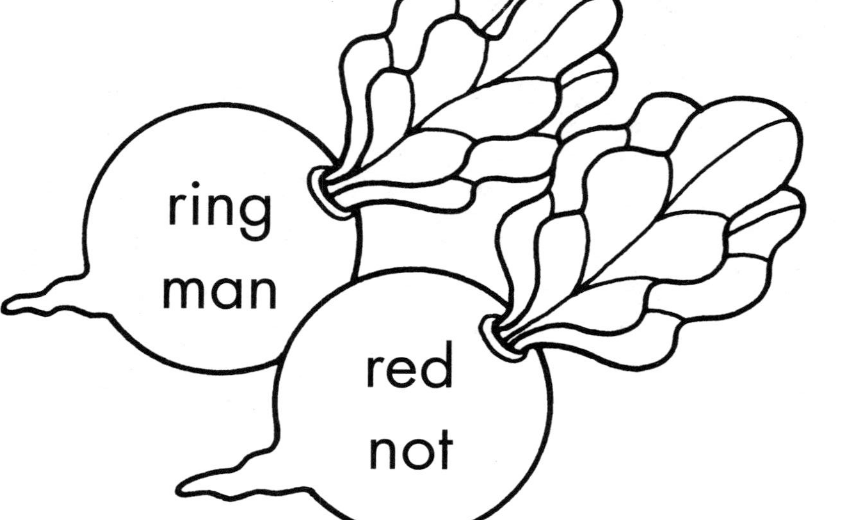

Name: ______________________________

Trace. Write.

S S S

Find each **S**. Color that shape gray. Then color the rest of the picture.

 Name: ______________________

Circle each **S**.

S J Z S

S C S G

Write **S** to complete the word.

___eagull

Color each item that begins with **S**.

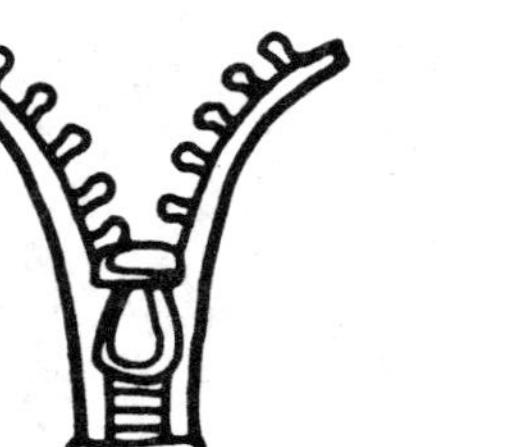

Name: ______________________

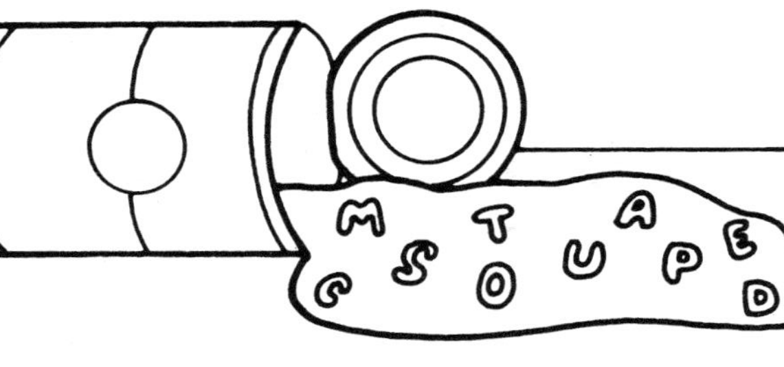

Trace.

s s s s

Write.

Circle each **s**.

j s z
s s

Find each **s**. Color that shape blue.
Then color the rest of the picture.

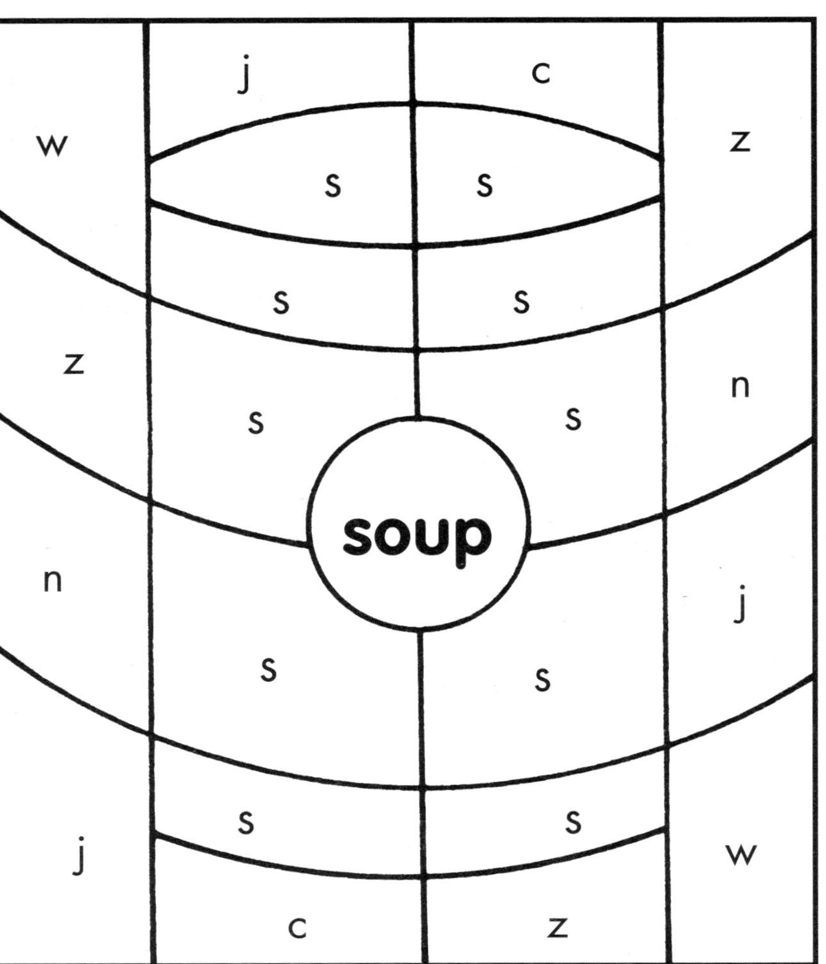

Name: ______________________

Color each **s** in the soup. Then write **s** two more times in the soup.

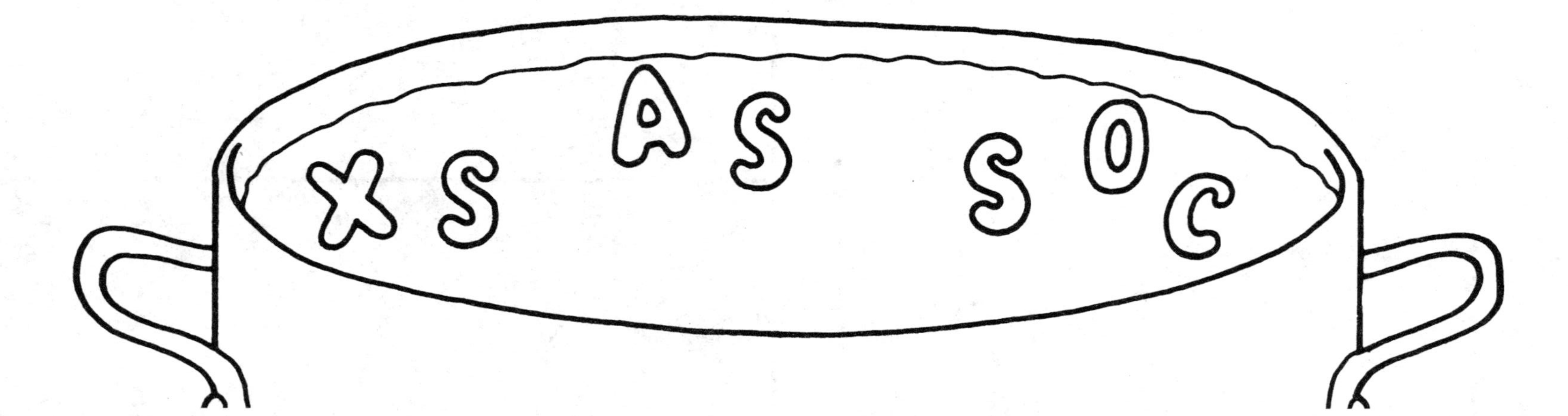

Trace the word below.
Read the words on the soup can.
Circle each word with an **s**.

soup

Name: ____________________

Trace.

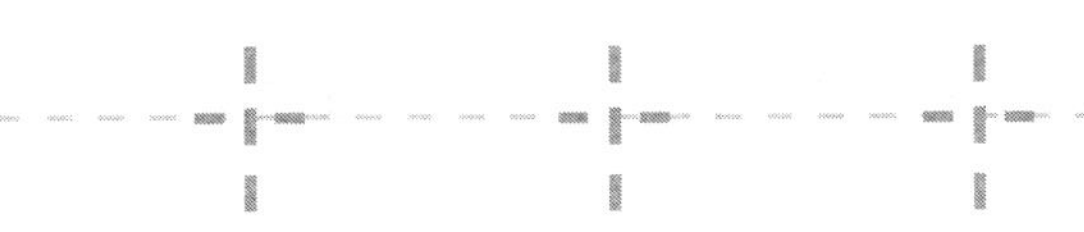

Write.

Circle each t.

Find each t. Color that shape green.
Then color the rest of the picture.

Name: ______________________

Trace each turtle. Write **t** one each one.

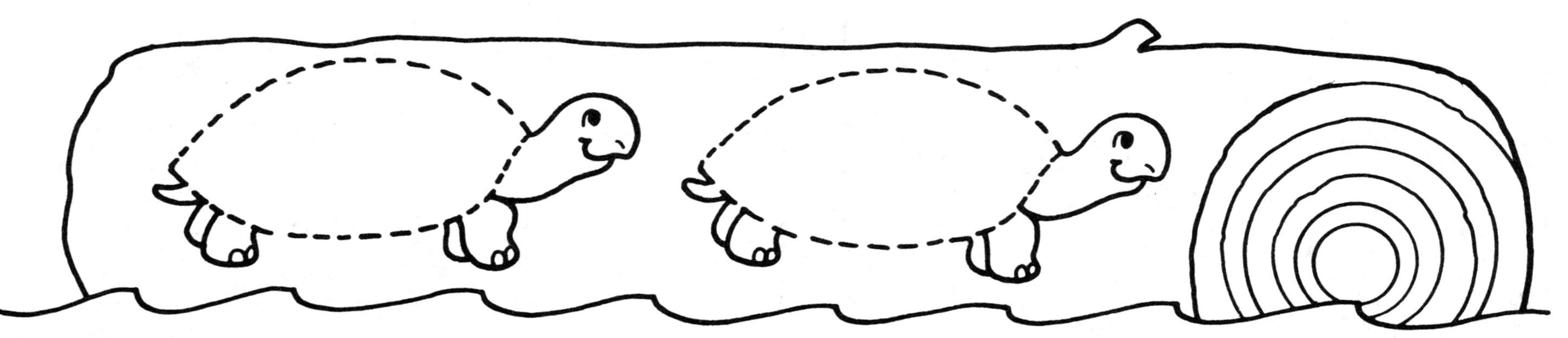

Trace the word below.
Read the words on the tent.
Circle each word with a **t**.

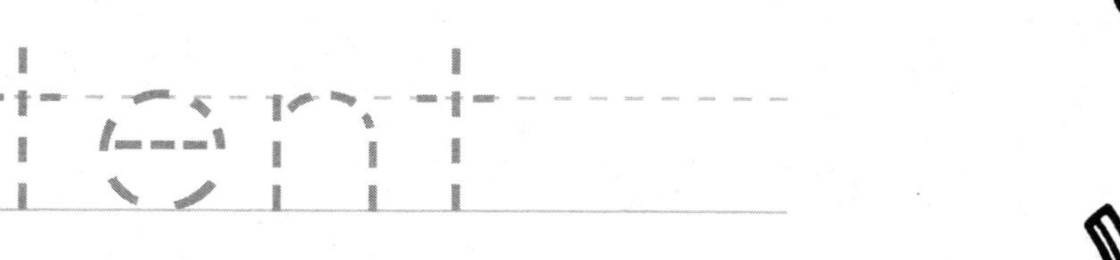

Name: ______________________

Trace. Write.

Find each **U**. Color that shape purple. Then color the rest of the picture.

Name: ______________________________

Circle each **U**.

U C U V

D U J U

Write **U** to complete the word.

_nicorn

Color each item that begins with **U**.

83 Name: ____________________

Trace.

u u u u

Write.

Circle each **u**.

a u u
n u

Find each **u**. Color that shape purple.
Then color the rest of the picture.

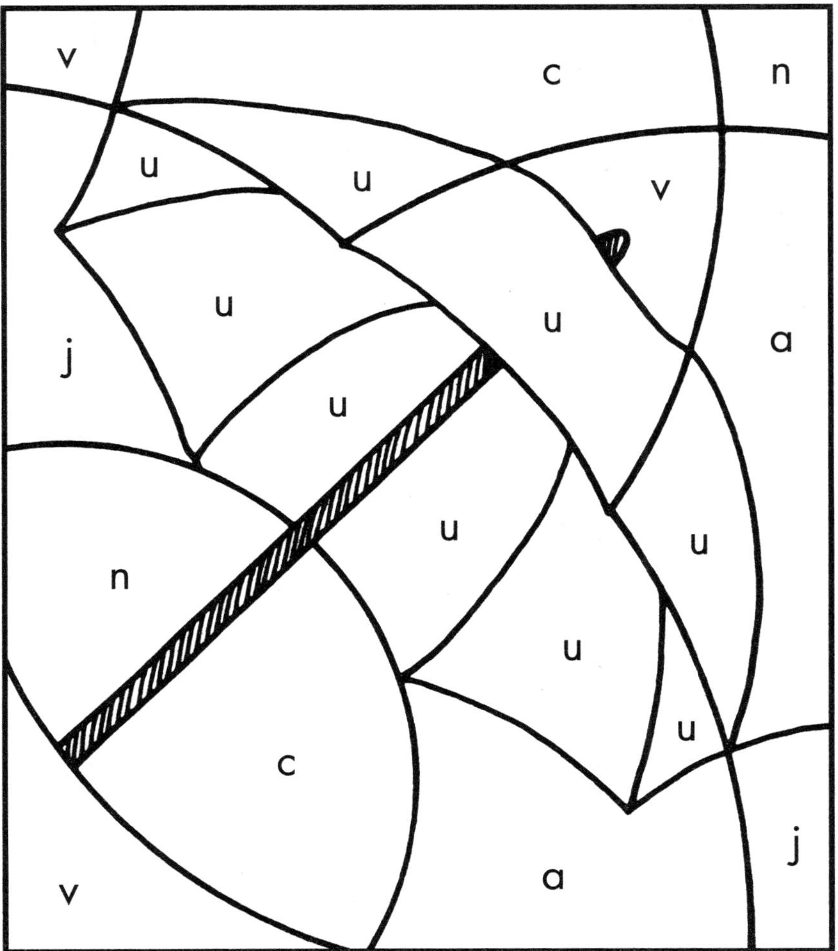

Name: ____________________

Trace each umbrella. Write **u** one each one.

Trace the word below.
Read the words on the umbrella.
Circle each word with a **u**.

85 Name: ____________________ Uppercase V

Trace. Write.

V V V

Find each **V**. Color that shape gray. Then color the rest of the picture.

Name: ____________________

Circle each **V**.

V M V Z

I V M V

Write **V** to complete the word.

ulture

Color each item that begins with **V**.

Name: ____________________

Trace.

Write.

Circle each **v**.

Find each **v**. Color that shape yellow.
Then color the rest of the picture.

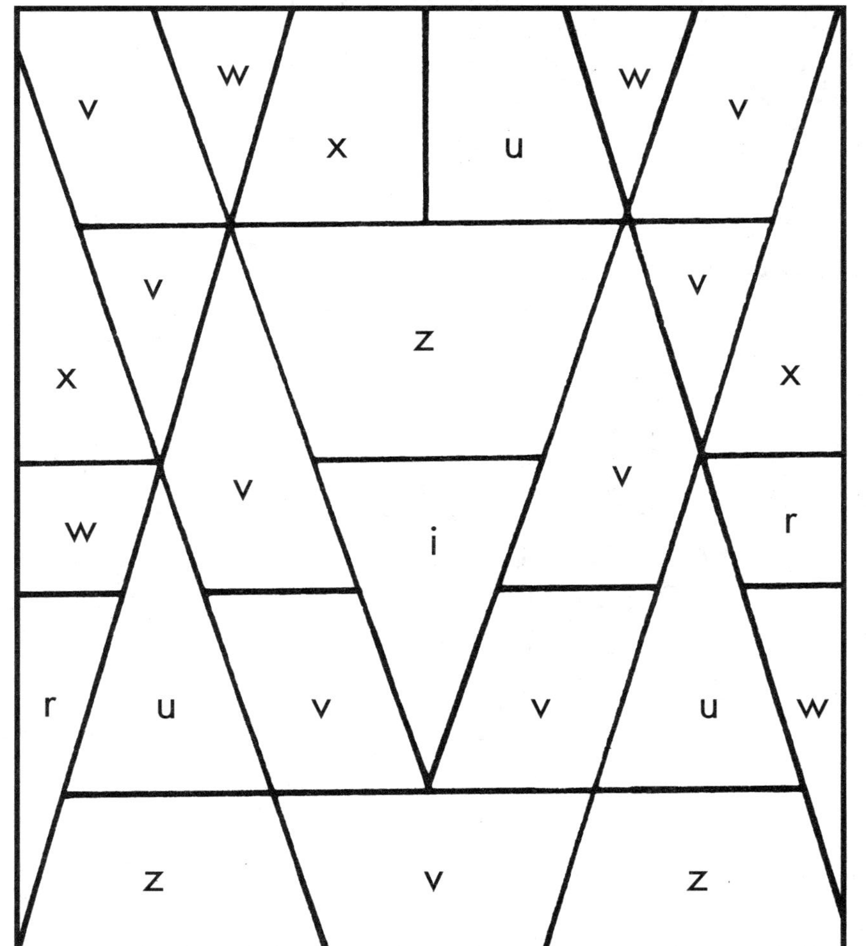

Name: ______________________

Trace each van. Write **v** on each one.

Trace the word below.
Read the words on the van.
Circle each word with a **v**.

van

89 Name: ______________________ Uppercase W

Trace. Write.

W W W

Find each **W**. Color that shape brown. Then color the rest of the picture.

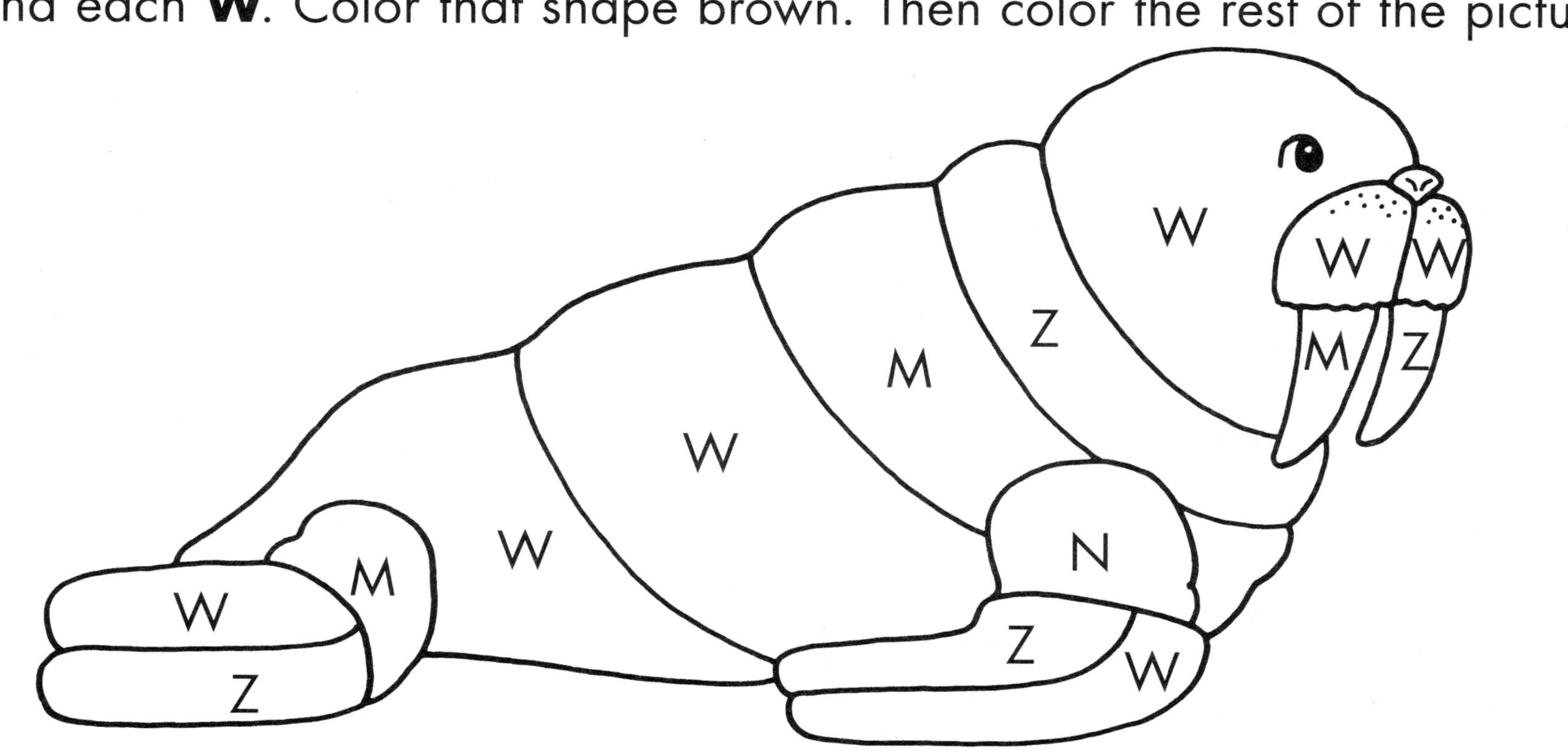

90 Name: ______________________ Uppercase W

Circle each **W**.

M W Z W

W N W M

Write **W** to complete the word.

_alrus

Color each item that begins with **W**.

Name: ____________________

Trace.

w w w w

Write.

Circle each **w**.

v w w
w z

Find each **w**. Color that shape blue.
Then color the rest of the picture.

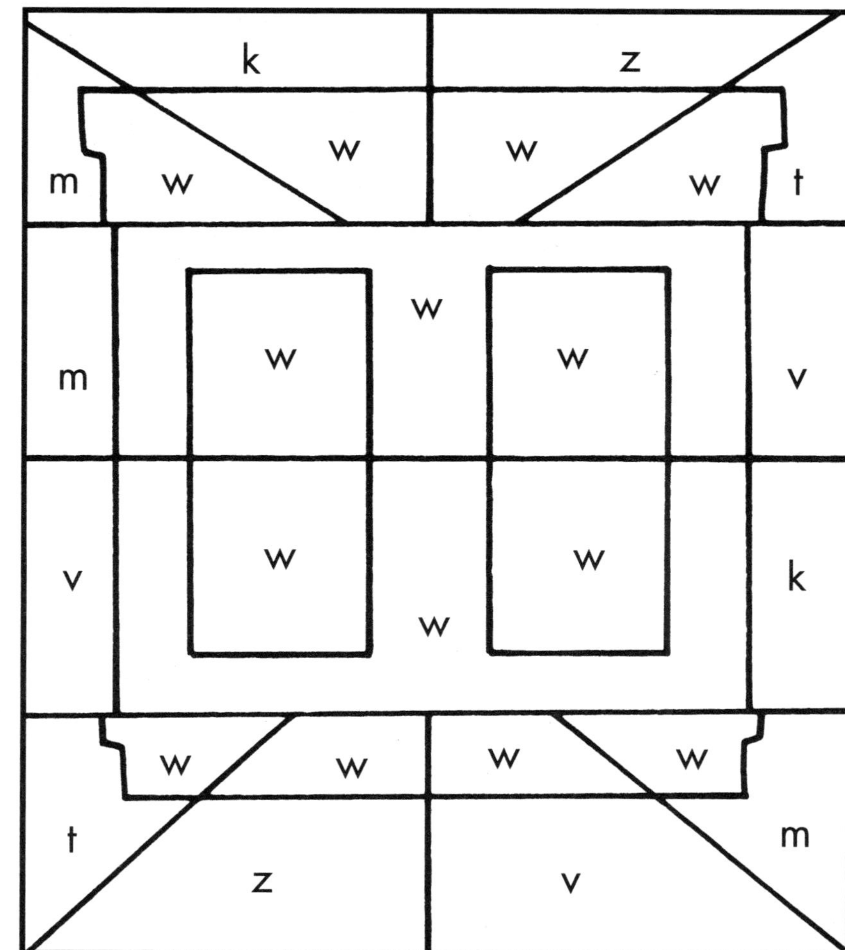

Name: ______________________

Draw another window for Walrus to wash. Write **w** on each window.

Trace the word below.
Read the words on the window.
Circle each word with a **w**.

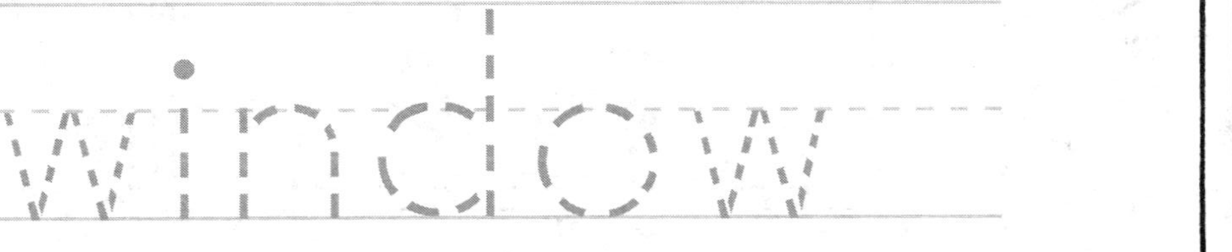

93 Name: ____________________

Trace. Write.

X X X

Find each **X**. Color that shape blue. Then color the rest of the picture.

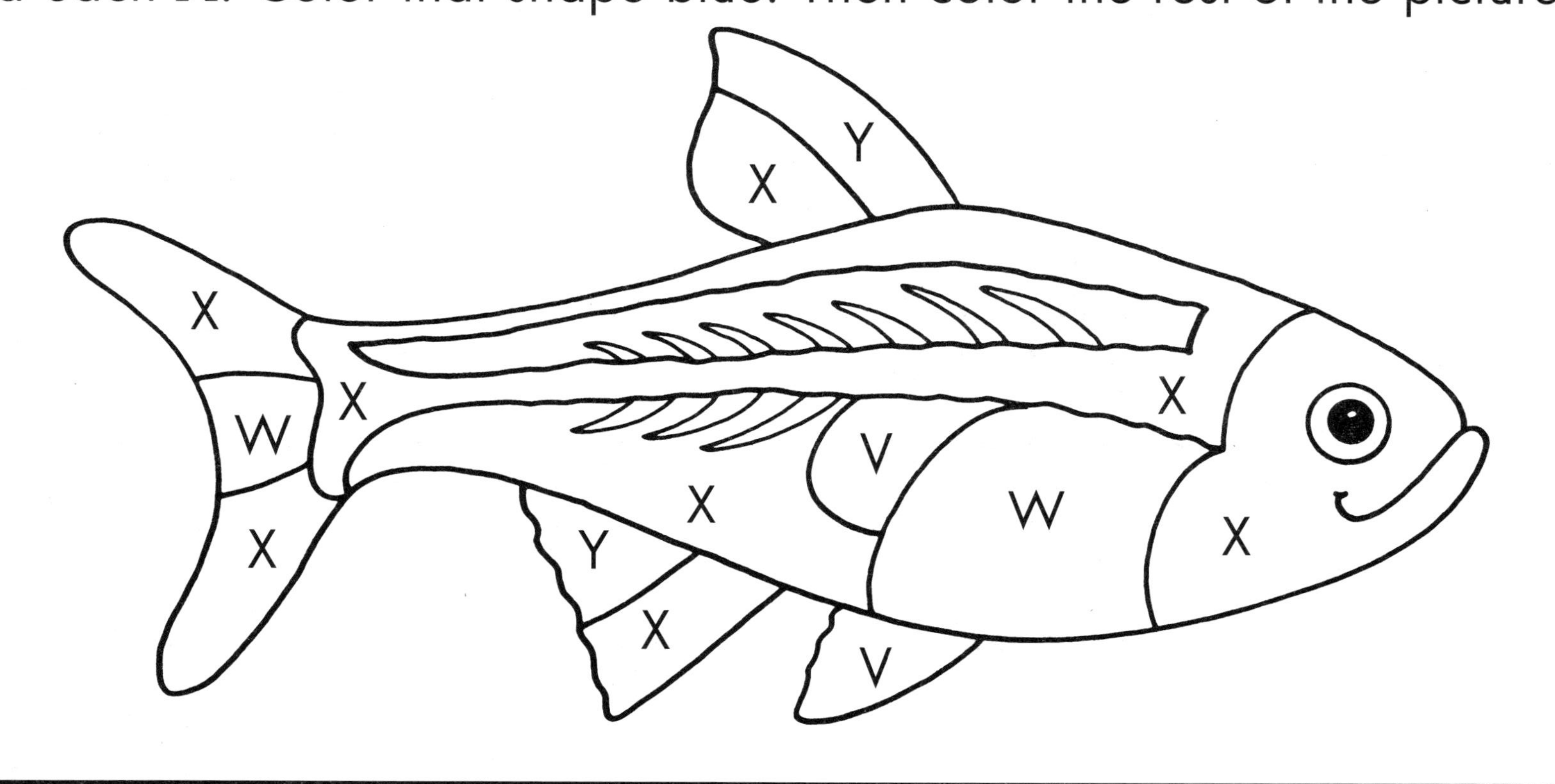

Name: ______________________

Circle each **X**.

W X Y X

X X Z W

Write **X** to complete the word.

_ray fish

Color each item that begins with the sound for **X**.

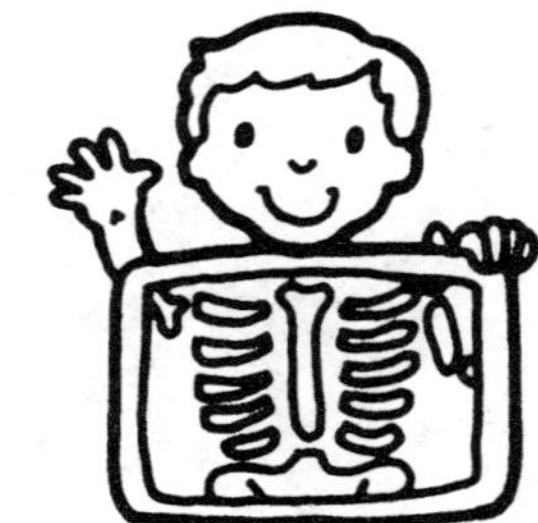

Trace.

Write.

Circle each **x**.

x y x
v x

Find each **x**. Color that shape blue.
Then color the rest of the picture.

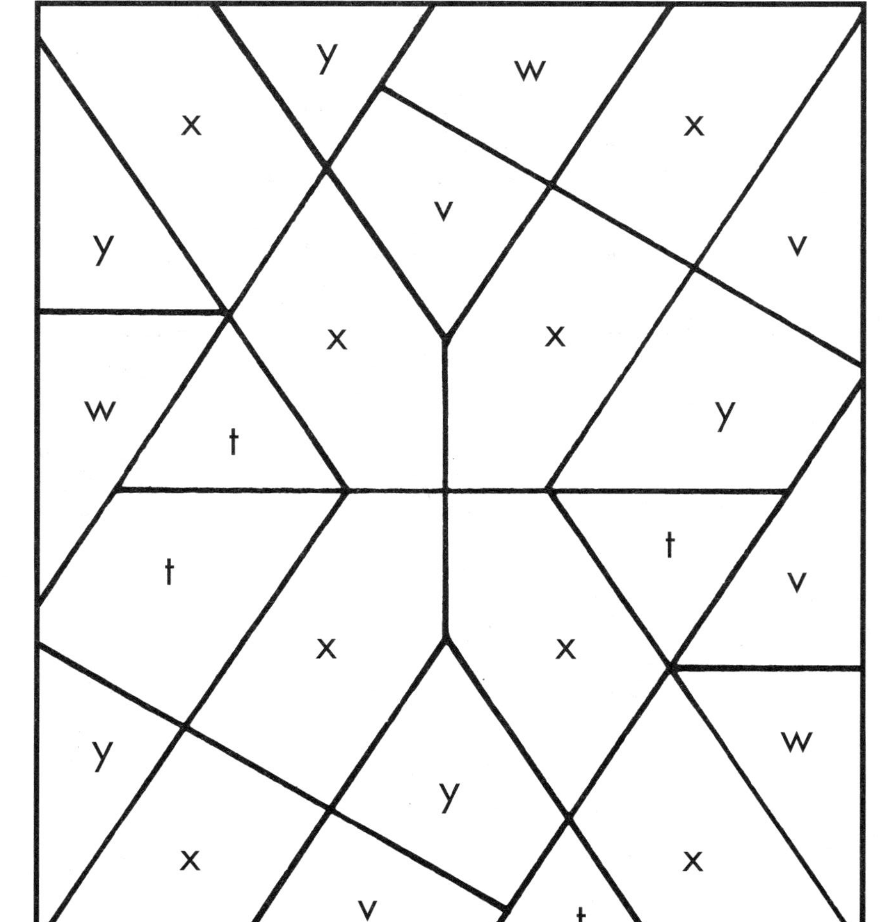

96 Name: ______________________

Lowercase x

Write **x** on each box.

Trace the word below.
Read the words on the box.
Circle each word with an **x**.

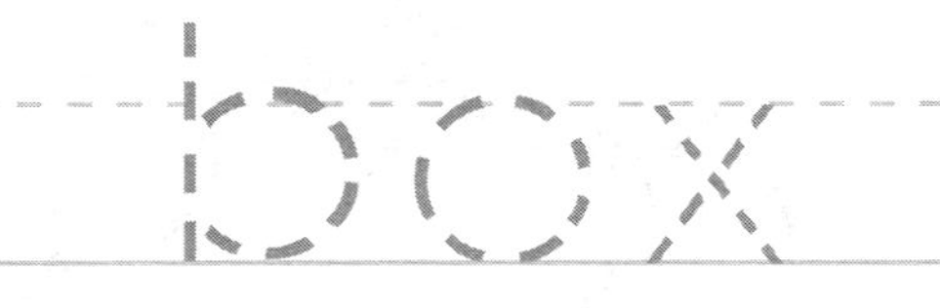

Name: ____________________

Trace. Write.

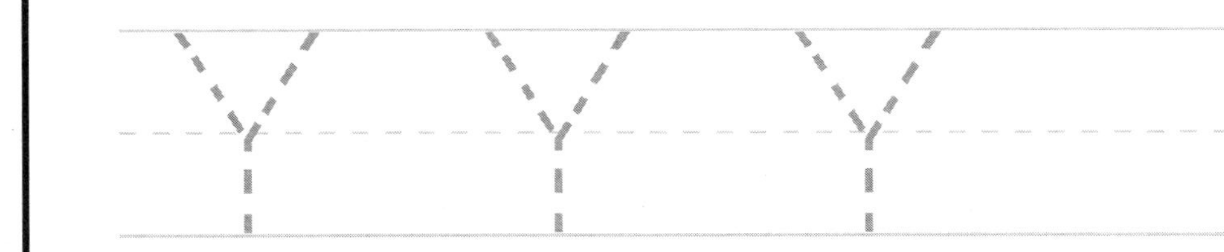

Find each **Y**. Color that shape brown. Then color the rest of the picture.

98 Name: ______________________ Uppercase Y

Circle each **Y**.

Y V Y N

V Y X Y

Write **Y** to complete the word.

_ak

Color each item that begins with **Y**.

99 Name: ____________________

Trace.

Write.

Circle each **y**.

Find each **y**. Color that shape yellow.
Then color the rest of the picture.

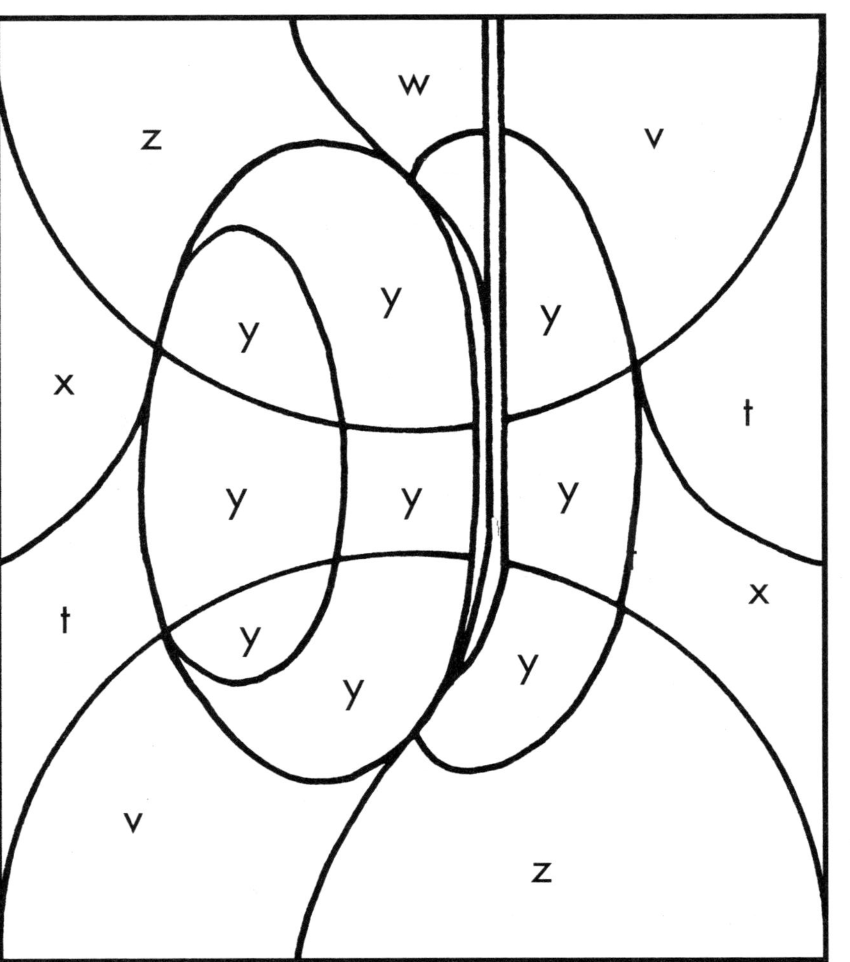

Name: ______________________

Write **y** on each yo-yo. Then color each one yellow.

Trace the word below.
Read the words on the yo–yos.
Circle each word with a **y**.

yo-yo

101 Name: ______________________________

Trace. Write.

Z Z Z

Find each **Z**. Color that shape black. Then color the rest of the picture.

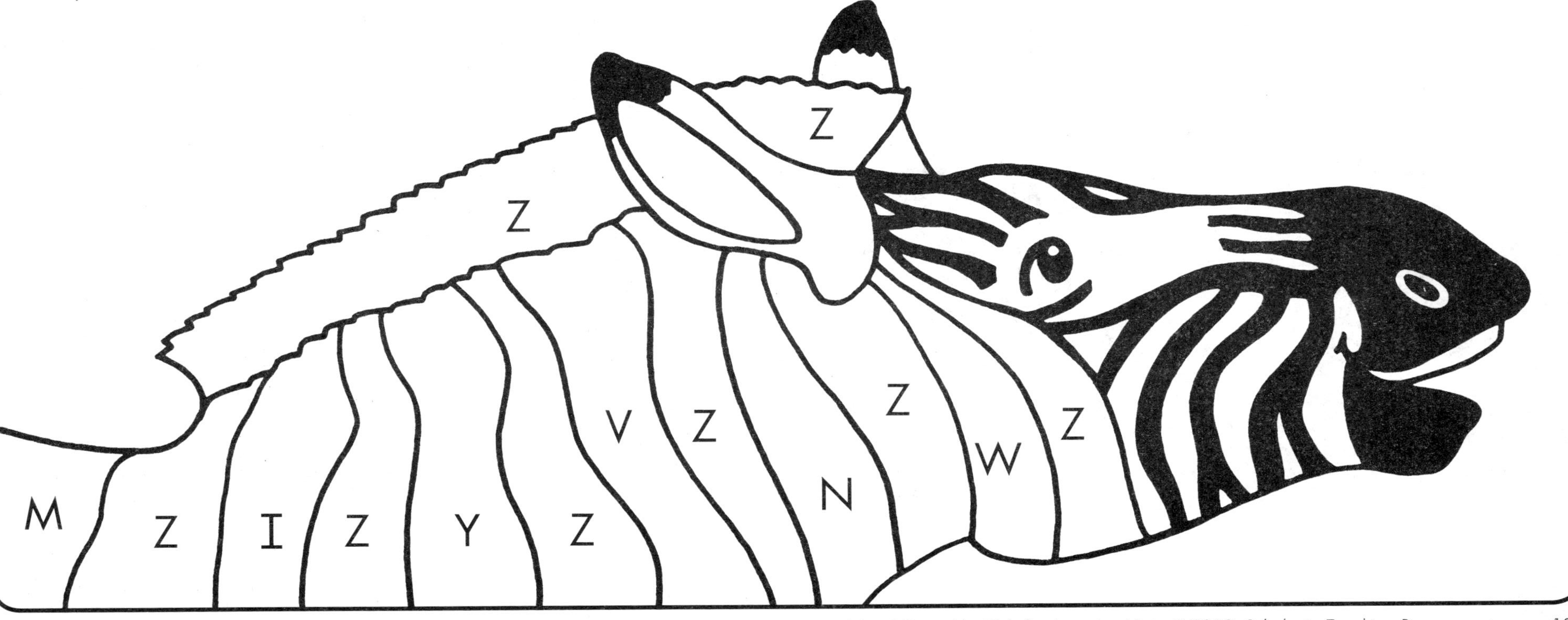

102 Name: ____________________

Uppercase Z

Circle each **Z**.

Z N I Z

M Z Z W

Write **Z** to complete the word.

ebra

Color each item that begins with **Z**.

Name: ______________________________

zebra

Trace.

z z z z

Write.

Find each **z**. Color that shape black. Then color the rest of the picture.

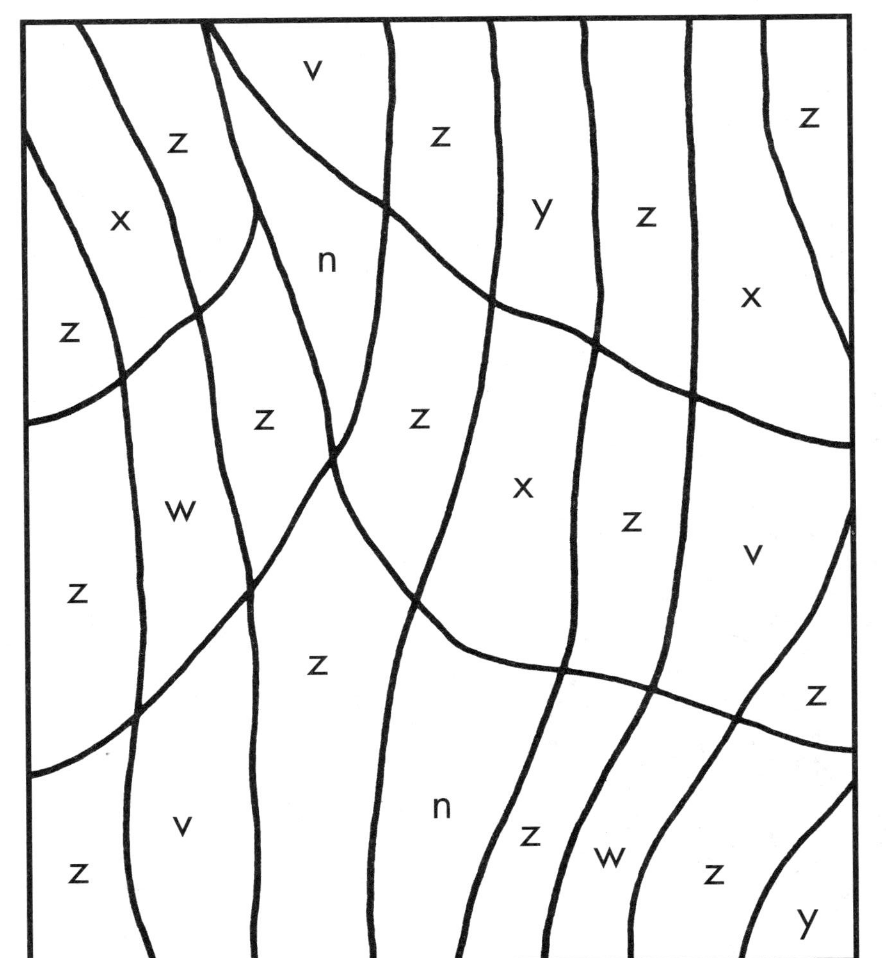

Circle each **z**.

z v z

z w

104 Name: ____________________ Lowercase z

Trace each zucchini. Write **z** on each one.

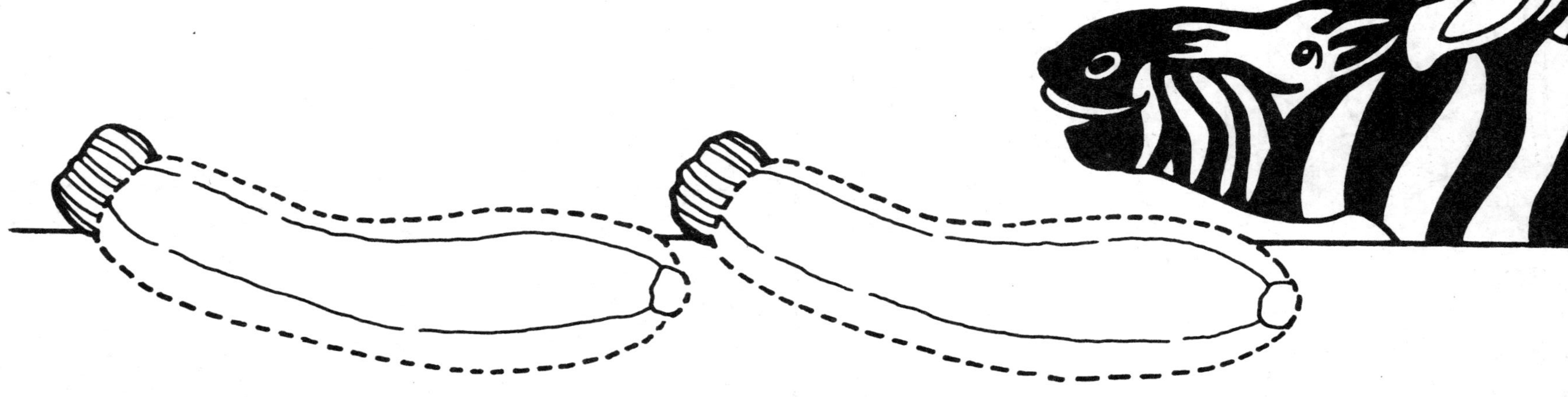

Trace the word below.
Read the words on the zoo.
Circle each word with a **z**.

zoo